Perfect Pie

by
Judith Thompson

Playwrights Canada Press
Toronto • Canada

Playwrights Canada Press
54 Wolseley Street, 2nd Floor
Toronto, Ontario CANADA M5T 1A5
(416) 703-0201 fax (416) 703-0059
cdplays@interlog.com http://www.puc.ca

Playwrights Canada Press acknowledges the support of The Canada Council for the Arts for our publishing programme and the Ontario Arts Council.

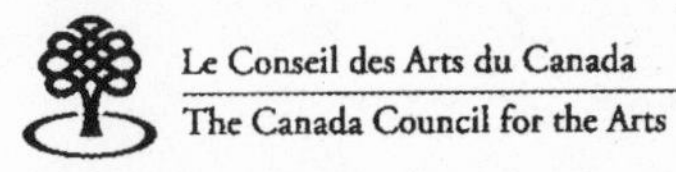

ONTARIO ARTS COUNCIL
CONSEIL DES ARTS DE L'ONTARIO

Cover photo by Cameron Wallace. Cover by Jodi Armstrong.

Canadian Cataloguing in Publication Data

Thompson, Judith, 1954-
Perfect Pie

A play
ISBN 0-088754-590-4

I. Title.

PS8589.H4883P47 2000 C812'.54 C99-933122-1
PR9199.3.T46P47 2000

First edition: May 2000. Second printing: February, 2001.
Printed and bound in Canada by Hignell Printing at Winnipeg, Manitoba.

Judith Thompson was born in 1954 in Montreal. She graduated from Queen's University in 1976 and graduated from the acting programme of The National Theatre School in 1979. At the age of 25, her first play *The Crackwalker,* was produced by Theatre Passe Muraille. Her work has won numerous awards and enjoyed great success internationally. She is a professor of Drama at University of Guelph and lives with her husband and five children in Toronto.

Dedication

This play is dedicated to my friend Jeannine (who never lived on a farm or won a pie contest).

Acknowledgements

I would like to thank Robert Sherrin, who commissioned the original monologue upon which this play is based, for his remarkable insight and dramaturgy.

I am indebted to Betty Ann Jordan for sharing with me the rich details of her childhood on a farm outside of Tweed, Ontario and to Shelagh O'Reilly for honouring me with the story of her horrific accident and the resulting six week coma.

There were two workshops of *Perfect Pie*, and I would like to thank everyone involved: Don Shipley, Katherine Kaszas, Iris Turcott, Fiona Reid, Nicola Cavendish, Jennifer Wigmore, Nancy Meckler, Tara Rosling, and Kristen Thomson, Kelli Fox and Severin Thompson.

Special thanks to Carolyn Azar, midwife to the text, who gave her heart and soul to this special *Perfect Pie*.

Introduction

> "Thoughts are the shadows of our feelings—always darker, emptier, and simpler".
>
> —*Friedrich Nietzsche*

Supernatural beings, Greek gods, and everyday ghosts have always envied humans for their ability to touch, to actually feel sensations. While we focus physical energy and mental concentration on hands and fingertips that can thread a needle or pick up a feather, the skin that covers our bodies is thoroughly sensitive to infinite degrees of sensation. Outline a letter or a child's back with your finger and she can learn to read it. How could we ever hope to put into words the response of skin to a warm bath or a gust of wind? Judith Thompson's plays have always attempted to make audiences feel that no sensation is trivial: the memory of an itchy shirt or a winter afternoon lasts a lifetime and connects us to an inner world of emotion that would not exist without the ability to remember the exact thrill of a first kiss or painful shock of a frozen toe. In *Perfect Pie,* smell and taste are thoroughly internalized sensations that are built in childhood to last a lifetime, the exact time of a living body. Every body has its own history. In moments of extraordinary power, the young Marie and Patsy experience the world of sensation together and establish through moments of friendship that we can share the knowledge of touch with each other, and that the most sacred form of human communication is granted through touch.

> "All art constantly aspires towards the condition of music".
>
> —*Walter Pater*

Science, philosophy, and the boredom of common sense have conspired to threaten the power of theatre to map out the full extent of human touch and human emotion. Judith brings theatre back to life by turning the pitch of emotion up loud. Since we have come to desensitize language, to control emotion, to name, contain, limit and distance, to be frightened of opera, poetry, emotion, and tears, Judith's music presents itself as the shock of direct contact. In the theatre of everyday life, the young Marie Begg is trapped by the forces who control language, turning it into a repressive apparatus for violence, pain, insult and social control. Patsy, herself a poet of touch and human contact, uses her friendship with Marie to escape the educational system that ultimately expresses itself in schoolyard bullying and the internal acts of omission and self-deceiving cruelty that turn us into respectable citizens. As an artist from day one, Marie's task is less self-realization than communication; those who suffer must find a language for themselves that would choke in the throats of the oppressors, while those of us who wander the earth at a distance from rape and violence might learn how to listen and feel. She will decide to change her name. In her direct experience of Marie's suffering, Patsy acquires a haunted life: "Stalker knows he would get me again... he knows that he can get me at any time he wants".

> Home's the place we head for in our sleep.
> Boxcars stumbling north in dreams
> don't wait for us. We catch them on the run.
>
> —*Louise Erdrich*

The magic of theatre is the magic of haunting—great actors accomplish something supernatural—but if you don't believe in the reality of ghosts beyond the stage, you will not detect the haunting of all human spaces. The long toil of human suffering hasn't disappeared without a trace, but it is the task of theatre to make sure that the traces you do find are vocal and physical. To believe in ghosts is to risk not being able to control their voices or your own. It is no secret that the everyday activity of funerals in North America have degenerated into awkward tea parties, with forced conversation about job prospects and cottage renovation and a strange collective sense that talking excessively about the dead may be in poor taste. We find ourselves with nothing to say or even without the need to say something, dreading sociability and longing for the solace of home with its promise of solitude and solitary pleasure and unobserved emotion. *Perfect Pie* began as a monologue concerned with imagining a life that might have been, feeling the burden of being close to someone who died before their time, robbed not just of life but of language, conversation, and the unfolding of an individual lifetime. Having reached a middle stage of her lifetime, Patsy remembers a friend who may have died or may have lived another life under another name; this was uncertain, and memory is in no way able to solve the problem of its own uncertainty. In its new, revised incarnation, *Perfect Pie* begins with an open letter, a call to memory from a place of contact: "I will not forget you, you are carved in the palm of my hand". When the play ends with these exact same words, the audience can fully accept the gift that has been offered them: haunting, the touch, feel, pain, emotion, and finally joy of memory.

—*Gregor Campbell*

Production History

Perfect Pie premiered at Tarragon Theatre, Toronto, Ontario.
January 11th - February 13th 2000.

Cast

PATSY	Nancy Palk
FRANCESCA	Sonja Smits
MARIE	Liisa Repo-Martell
PATSY (young)	Tara Rosling

Directed by Judith Thompson

Set and Costume Design	Sue LePage
Lighting Design	Andrea Lundy
Composition/Sound Design	Bill Thompson
Stage Management	Winston Morgan
Assistant Director	Caroline Azar

Act One, Scene One

Darkness. PATSY WILLET is in the kitchen of her farmhouse, at an old wooden table, making dough for a rhubarb pie. Moonlight illuminates a perfect ball of dough, a pot of tea and a teacup. There is a small tape recorder in front of her on the table. She is preparing to send a letter by tape to her old estranged friend, MARIE. She kneads the dough for a while. A train whistle sounds. She looks up at the window to glimpse the train. The train approaches, and passes.

PATSY "I will not forget you, you are carved in the palm of my hand."

Dawn breaks. She presses "Record" on the Tape Recorder.

Marie? Are you sitting down? Cause if you're not I think you better cause you might just get the dizzies when you find out who I am. Now don't turn me off thinkin' I'm some kinda crazy stranger like one of your fans. Because although I am a fan, I am not crazy I don't think, and I'm not a stranger that is for sure... I am... it's funny I feel a little shy to say, because I'm sure you know who I am at this point, at least I hope you know: that I am Patsy. *(Pause)* Willet. Now Patsy McAnn but you would know me as Willet. You know? Of course you do: Big red face, hash brown hair? We hung around together near Marmora, Ontario like Siamese Twins till you left town when you were about fifteen or sixteen? Well Marie I have followed your career of course; and I am proud... to have known you, Marie. And, well, the reason that I am gettin' in touch with you after all this time, Marie, this thirty some years is I have been... yearning. To... behold you, I suppose. Because I'll be honest with you, when I have been having a hard day and I'm very tired and it's the end of the day and I'm makin' supper or doin' the dishes and the room fills with oh orange light and I hear the train, the low whistle at the back of our property and I stare out the window and I see – just the glimpse of it, of the train speeding on to Montreal, the crash... does flash out, in my mind; like a sheet; of lightning, and when the flash is over, and all is dark again, I know you did not survive. I know in my heart you did not survive, Marie. So how is it? How is it that I see you there, out there, in the world?

PATSY goes to get Rhubarb Fruit Pie filling from fridge and fills the pie shell.

Scene Two

Light on MARIE/FRANCESCA, in her own dark apartment in the Big City, a great view of the city at night behind her. She remembers...

Scene Three

MARIE and PATSY, (Young), in white sing the 1st verse of "Abide with Me".

MARIE/ PATSY

Abide with Me... Fast falls the eventide
The darkness deepness; *(Pause)*
Lord
with me abide:
When other helpers fail, and comforts
flee,
Help of the helpless...

Scene Four

FRANCESCA stares out into the darkness.She smells the pie and takes a fingerful and eats it.

PATSY

Well, Marie, I got all my chickens waitin' to be fed and the damn cows to take care of– they been gorging on crabapples so they're in agony with the gas, eh, bloated up just terrible so I better let you go; Oh I almost forgot. Hope the pie's not too crushed out; it's a fresh rhubarb, Marie; grown in my own garden. My prize winner at the Northumberland County Pie Contest. Makes a really nice light dessert. So just heat it up and serve it to your man, if you have one of those in your life, which I am sure you likely do. Marie, I'll let you go now, if you haven't turned me off already, and ahh listen: if you do happen to be drivin' east, to Ottawa or Montreal... please... go on to highway seven. You know the way from there; past the Big Red Apple and down the road a few miles and just show up at my door. I'll put the kettle on and we'll have a visit. So I know you're still... here. In the world. Would you? Would you ever think of doin' that?

All best, Your old friend, Patsy.

PATSY presses the STOP button on the recorder.

Scene Five

The two GIRLS sing the second verse of "Abide with Me".

2nd verse.

MARIE/ PATSY Swift to it's close
ebbs out life's little day;
Earth's joys grow dim,
it's glories pass away;
Change and decay
in all around I see...

Scene Six

Marie, now FRANCESCA on railroad tracks. She is re–visiting the site; perhaps in reality, before she goes to see PATSY, perhaps in her imagination. When PATSY speaks, she speaks from her kitchen. They are in an abstract dialogue: actually PATSY is listening to FRANCESCA's tape, sent some time before the visit. PATSY completes her pie and puts it in the oven.

FRANCESCA Patsy? It's me... yeahhh. Well... Hellooooo – doesn't seem a big enough word... does it...? After all this time. Hearing your voice... made something inside me... I don't know, bloom; like the crabapples on your farm; I somehow always, but never... expected... to hear your voice again. I have thought about you so much over the years, Patsy. It's funny, as I... erased more and more of Marmora I remembered... more and more of you. The tips of your eyelashes. Every freckle on your arm. Your face: so clear to me! And I would have known your voice anywhere. Anywhere. I've often listened for it, you know, and even thought I've heard it, not just in Toronto, but in far away places: in the Munich Train station once I was SURE I heard your voice I turned and of course, not you and I – oh I *yearn*, Patsy, to see you again.

PATSY Course I've seen you a few times on the TV, and in the newspaper but it's not the same. As face to face. And although you are lookin' well in the sense of, very attractive for your age, Marie, you are lookin'–

FRANCESCA –It was very strange to hear the name "Marie" you know, "Marie... Begg"... feels to me like a reproach somehow; a weird sister I have dogchained in the attic...

PATSY –Not – well – in the face somehow, and I am very concerned about this Marie–

FRANCESCA –Thank you so so much for the prize winning pie. It was inexpressibly delicious; I ate the whole thing myself, in the dark. I gorged on that delicious pastry while listening to your voice. Every bite was perfect; I could almost taste your hands in the pastry. But you always did make good pastry. I can just imagine you kneading the dough the way you used to. With that almost ferocious look...

In unison.

FRANCESCA On your – face

PATSY Because I care about your face.

PATSY I see it, sometimes, in the kitchen window, early in the morning when I get up to make my dough.

FRANCESCA I'm ashamed of how little I remember... of my life in Marmora. It's like one of those vast intrinsicate dreams.

PATSY –And it's always while I'm makin' my dough I get thinkin' of things you know, I'm looking out at the roseate dawn and the mist... *(the following lines are somewhat overlapped)*

PATSY And I think of the time

FRANCESCA that all but disappears

PATSY We woke up.

FRANCESCA when you wake up...

PATSY We were both in these softy soft flannel pajamees and you woke me up and you said, "look" and I look out the window and I saw all this...

FRANCESCA Ice.

PATSY Glistening, Shimmering, Crystalline–

FRANCESCA Ice.

PATSY Glazing the trees, the bushes, the barn roof, and the fields all the way down to the Dark blue lake.

FRANCESCA Yes, I remember, and all the icicles...

PATSY And I would like... Grab your hand and we shove on the rubber boots and we are out the door and we go! We slide, all over the farm in our boots and our nighties laughin' and–

FRANCESCA –Sliding, across the fields, sliding and shrieking!

PATSY And the AIR!

FRANCESCA Oh, the air!

PATSY I think of those times.

FRANCESCA I think of those times–

PATSY Early in the morning.

FRANCESCA Late at night

PATSY When I get up to make my dough...
So if you are comin' over this way...

FRANCESCA And my heart races.

PATSY You might want to see your old friend.

FRANCESCA I am... somewhat shy of Marmora. But I would like very much to see you, Patsy.

PATSY I won't go in to Toronto. I went once to see "The Phantom". Ric took me for my birthday but I did not care for it at all. No. You're gonna have to come to me, Marie.

FRANCESCA has arrived in PATSY's domain.

FRANCESCA Yes.

Scene Seven

FRANCESCA is now in PATSY's kitchen, late morning. They have a moment, which is the first moment they encounter each other.

FRANCESCA Oh yes. It is exactly the same.... As I remember. This wallpaper. Those little bluebirds, and the vines.

FRANCESCA runs her hands along the wallpaper. PATSY watches her.

PATSY Right in style in 1929. If ya try to scrape it off the whole wall comes down. Hah. I'd like to gut the kitchen but Ric keeps puttin' it off.

FRANCESCA Oh but the... history is wonderful, don't you think?

PATSY You sound like my Mum. I say, "Tear the history down, and give it a nice coat of paint." See that Peanuts comic strip? Over there? That was up before you left, I am talkin' thirty–five years. I said to Mum, I said, "Mum, if you care about the strip, Take it down, and put it inside the family photo album for Pete's sake." She said "no", she liked it on the wall it reminded her of Dad. Because he had found it funny. It was one of the few times he laughed right out loud, ever. She said if she put it in a photo album she wouldn't never get it out. So I haven't had the heart to take it down. If I touch it, it will turn to dust.

FRANCESCA When did your father die?

PATSY Ahhhh...I guess it was about – five or no, six years ago. He was seventy-eight years old. Still working the farm every day. He'd been raking leaves. Just out front there. My mother was right here, scrapin' egg off a fry pan, when it happened.

FRANCESCA Heart?

PATSY nods.

PATSY He just fell over the bag of leaves.

FRANCESCA It must have been very hard on your mother.

PATSY They'd been married for fifty years, eh? She tried, right? To keep going with her church work and that, you know the kind of person she was, always doin' for others, but you could see the strain. Little things. Like she didn't wipe down her counters the same.

Scene Eight

Past.

FRANCESCA as MARIE, about eight, standing in the schoolyard, against a wall. Her head is very itchy, as she has lice. PATSY, with jumping rope approaches. She is very interested in the new, "poor" girl. She stares at her. MARIE does not look at PATSY.

PATSY Hullo. *(MARIE does not respond)*

PATSY What's your name again? I didn't really hear ya when you said it in class.

MARIE Marie Begg.

PATSY Pardon? You're talkin' so softy soft.

MARIE Marie. Begg.

PATSY Oh! That's a beautiful name. Like olden days.

MARIE I hate it.

PATSY *(gasp)* You shouldn't say you hate your name.

MARIE Why not?

PATSY Because if you say you hate your name you're saying you hate your mother because Your mother gave you that name and you shouldn't say you hate your mother. MARIE BEGGS.

MARIE Begg. Marie Begg.

PATSY Oh. I still think it's a beautiful name.

MARIE finally turns to look at PATSY.

Scene Nine

Present.

FRANCESCA I always loved this house. I always felt... comfortable here.

PATSY Ric's been fixing it up, slowly. He's handy, you know, but he is a real procrastinator, I mean there is so much...

FRANCESCA Oh I think it's wonderful just the way it is. Perfect.

PATSY Oh but it's falling down, Marie. It has been for the last thirty years. Dad, he just didn't have the time–

FRANCESCA Your Dad was a lovely man. I remember he used to tell jokes in that gentle voice while he was milking the cows by hand. He would lay his cheek against the cow and then he would look right at you and...

PATSY plugs the kettle in for tea.

PATSY We were one of the last to get in the machinery, about 1963.

FRANCESCA He was... traditional.

PATSY He was cheap!

FRANCESCA And his hands, were so... strong, remember? Remember he would pick us both up and.... Didn't he used to... slice open the cows? To relieve their gas? When you mentioned on the tape about the cows being bloated with gas I had a flash... of your dad with a very sharp tool, slicing....

PATSY Oh yes, we still do it in emergencies, Marie. See, the poor things are in agony from the overeating. Every spring it happens, after the long winter in the barn, eh? They start gorgin' on the alfalfa. The gas'll kill em you know. Oh yeah, you have to know exactly where to slice, which stomach, and with a clean knife.

FRANCESCA looks at a laminated picture on the fridge of Ric and the boys and Patsy.

FRANCESCA What a beautiful family you are. The boys have your eyes, Patsy. Oh he looks adorable.

PATSY *(she gets up, bustles)* They should be back from the fair in Dundee around suppertime if you can stay that long; Ric's dying to see you again, I been talkin' about you so much...

FRANCESCA Well...

PATSY And I think Kevy may be coming home with a red ribbon for Blossom, she's the Jersey we gave to him for his 4H eh, he's done very well with her. You will like Kevin, he is the image of my father ...And Ry is shy, you know reserved, but once you get to know him? He is the funniest, I'm serious, the wittiest boy. He could do very well in the stand-up comedy.

FRANCESCA I'm sorry, I really do have to be off by six or so.

PATSY Oh right, your big "gala" in Montreal. I'm sorry, I forgot. Stupid.

An awkward moment.

FRANCESCA I would absolutely love to stay and meet your family. I never enjoy these events, but... it's kind of in my honour.

PATSY Stupid of me to forget.

FRANCESCA No no no. I just wish... well....

PATSY So what time did you say you need to be there?

FRANCESCA If I'm there by 9:00 or so... that should be fine.

PATSY Well it's a good four hours. So if I were you, I would leave by 5:00 sharp. But then I like to be punctual. Now you, you used to be late for everything. Always marked tardy on your report cards, remember? Are you still that way?

FRANCESCA Well–

PATSY –It really is too bad you won't meet the boys.

FRANCESCA Yes. I would really love to... sometime.

PATSY Maybe on the way back.

FRANCESCA Sure. Yes, maybe.

Uncomfortable silence.

Music.

PATSY Well...

PATSY pours Tea. Music over awkward moment.

The baking bell goes off.

PATSY Oh. There's my baking.

FRANCESCA Smells wonderful.

PATSY Well, you know what that is, eh?

Scene Ten

Past.

Schoolyard.

MARIE scratches her head while looking at the ground.

PATSY Where you come from anyways?

MARIE Detroit.

PATSY In the States? You come from the States? Oh my gosh I love the States. The States is fancy!

MARIE No.... .. NO. Like we're from here. My dad he grew up here but then they lost the Farm, cause our well run dry and so he went to work makin' cars in Detroit like his cousins but he hurt his back and my Gramma took a stroke an left us the house so we come back that's all. He's workin' as a hand over at Penny's cattle ranch near Tweed but he grew up here. We're from here.

PATSY So what's it like in the States? Is it really fun?

MARIE Their chocolate bars are better.

PATSY Really? What's your favourite?

MARIE Zagnut.

PATSY "Zagnut." Cool. ZAGNUT. How old are you?

MARIE Nine. My birthday was in August. August 23rd. We went to the Dairy Queen.

PATSY Oh my GOSH mine is January 23rd! That's amazing. Maybe you could come to my birthday party. We'll be going skating on the river. Would you like to? Would you like to come? Marie? Cuz we're gonna do lots of other fun stuff too like um musical chairs? We'll play musical chairs and my mother, she plays the piano? And sings like this really cool song about this pretty girl who is on her way to a party? And it's like really cold like a hundred below zero and so she like falls asleep in the snow and she freezes in her Sleighride thing? And my mother? She's singin' and then when she stops? Like you have to sit in a chair, and...

PATSY jumps into a "freeze" position. MARIE expresses acceptance, joy.

Scene Eleven

Present.

Kitchen: PATSY transfers the cookies to a plate to cool.

FRANCESCA Gumdrop cookies!

PATSY You're favourite! Soon as we walked in the house it was, "Did your mom make those gumdrop cookies?" "Do you think we could have one?" Or two? Or three? And you would take as many as you could get in your little hands–

FRANCESCA –Oh oh. Ohhhh. There is nothing, nothing like the smell of gumdrop cookies in your kitchen. I could honestly give up everything for it... It's what I want to smell as I lay dying, you know, in a nursing home or on the 401 or a wet field after a lightning storm. I remember sometimes your mother would let us hand her the gumdrops, to rest in the cookie batter. "I'd like a yellow drop now please." she would say.

PATSY Poor Mum. After Dad passed away she was dead within 16 months eh? Cancer of the kidneys. She used to lie on that divan right there, all day. It was my Grandmother's.

FRANCESCA Yeah, I remember it.

Pause.

PATSY Dark green bile coming out of her mouth and the morphine didn't touch that pain Marie it was like hyena dogs eating her body, eating her alive, day after day, night after night and there is nothing we can do. Well one day the pain seems to have subsided, eh. And we're feelin' kinda hopeful, we are all in her hospital room, 'cept Wayne and Roger of course, eatin' her chocolates, readin' the paper, I'm changin' the water in her vases thinkin' how rancid that smells when she takes, like a convulsion. Her face like twists like rubber and her body goes rigid and I start screamin'. Marie, they had to strong-arm me out of the room. This was my mother. I kneeled down in the waiting room and I prayed. I prayed so hard to God I went purple. I was certain that she would pull through because I had always believed in the power of prayer and I felt the presence of God, I felt His breath on my face and I was sure... I was sure he would breathe her to LIFE and there's people running in and out and then my Aunt Nancy, with a line down her face and her black coat over her arm... she is standing there and at first I thought she was gonna say "Mum is fine, she is okay and and we're gonna take her home" and I thought thank you God thank you for this and then I saw her face. Her eyes, like her pupils these large black holes; And then I knew; I knew I was stupid, simple to think Mum would make it out of there alive and in that moment, I wondered, Marie, if there is any God at all "See I will not forget you are carved in the palm of my hand." That's what the minister said at her funeral. I liked that, I liked that very much.

Schoolbell.

Scene Twelve

Past.

MARIE crouches. She is afraid to go back into school, past the taunting children.

PATSY Are you scared cause they were teasin' you before?

MARIE I'm not goin' back.

PATSY Don't mind them they're just ignorant.

MARIE Not going back there.

PATSY You go back in with me and they won't dare say nothing more. They say something? I report them to Mr. Eaves. You know the principal? With the glass eye? He's really really nice. *(pause)* And if I report them? They'll get the strap. Cause Mr. Eaves comes to our house for Christmas dinner. Always has seconds of stuffing. And oh my goodness, you should see that strap. Gerry d'Entremont got it for blowin' his nose on his desk? And he said Mr.Eaves smiled the whole time he was strapping him. And you know what he was smilin' at?

PATSY looks up at imaginary picture. MARIE also looks.

The picture of the Queen.

MARIE The Queen? Of England? She's hardly pretty.

PATSY I know. My mother even met her. In Belleville? She curtseyed to her.

School bell rings again.

MARIE Your mother met the Queen?

Scene Thirteen

Present.

FRANCESCA I knew that my mother was dying. My Aunt Trudy tracked me down. Begged me to come. Back here. To Marmora. I stayed on my bed for days; didn't leave my apartment until I knew she was dead.

PATSY I still go to church, you know, I sit there, I even sing in the choir, but I don't really believe anymore. Not after that.

Silence.

FRANCESCA No. I don't know. Sometimes I do.

PATSY When? When do ya?

FRANCESCA After a stomach flu. You know... that moment when you've been – sitting up all night in bed with the pain, running to the bathroom, throwing up bile, passing out while you throw up, drinking almost a whole bottle of antacid and endless cups of hot water, and just trying to bear it and just when I think I really cannot stand it any longer, when I think I will just decompose with the pain, the pain... lifts. And I believe in God again.

PATSY Oh to me that's just the devil playin' with you. Because you know that stomach flu is comin' back. And you also know it may turn to stomach cancer one day, right? And then it will go on for months like that till you die! Stomach flu's just a preview, right?

FRANCESCA *(laughs)* Patsy. You haven't changed at all.

PATSY No. I'm exactly the same. On the other hand, I'm totally different. Like you. Hey. Have a cookie. Go on. Gorgeous.

FRANCESCA Thank you. Oh. Patsy. They are heaven. HEAVen.

PATSY Hm. You talk so... different. Than you did. I mean, of course, that's to be expected.

FRANCESCA Sorry. Am I sounding very–

PATSY I'm listening for Marie, right?

FRANCESCA And... have you heard her yet?

PATSY *(long pause)* In the... *(PATSY illustrates with her hands)* undertow.

Scene Fourteen

Both GIRLS on swing, having big fun. They jump off in a thrill of laughter.

PATSY Are you poor?

MARIE No.

PATSY You look poor.

MARIE No I don't.

PATSY I mean only a little. Just the scabs on your legs. That IS a nice dress. I like the zipper. Is that what they're wearing in the States? Is that what's in style?

MARIE shrugs.

Scene Fifteen

Present.

Kitchen: PATSY wraps the remaining cookies, and starts making lunch.

PATSY You know my brother Wayne, right? You remember what a sweet kid he was? He comes for my mum's funeral with the town whore on his arm.

FRANCESCA You have a "Town Whore"?

PATSY Well. She is very loose. And what is she got around her dirty little neck but my mother's cultured pearl necklace.

FRANCESCA I remember that necklace.

PATSY He just went into the house and into her dresser and put mum's pearls round this little whore's neck. I don't know what he was trying to pull.

FRANCESCA Well coming to your mother's funeral with the "Town Whore" is better than not coming at all.

Pause as she puzzles at her selfishness.

PATSY Maybe you just weren't ready for this place. You know, didn't dare to look back. Afraid you'd turn to stone like what's her name in the Greek Mythology. That's what I been tellin' myself all these years, anyways, about you.

FRANCESCA is puzzled.

PATSY Why you woulda done what you did.

FRANCESCA Abandoned you.

PATSY When I woke up from a coma first thing I say, I go, "Where's Marie? Where's Marie?" I mean I didn't know if you were even alive until I read about you in the paper, ten years later.

Past

FRANCESCA remembers. MARIE, her hands high in the air, concentrates and speaks, sending her thoughts to PATSY.

MARIE Dear dear dear dear dearest friend Patsy, I am sending you this letter by thought because I do not want to contaminate you with my scabby voice or my messy handwriting. I am sending you this letter by thought to tell you that I will not be bothering you ever again. Not you, nor anyone in Marmora, so fear not, my friend. You will not even see my shadow again. I know that it is not possible that you would ever ever ever accept my apology so I say "I am Sorry" for the train with no expectation that you will forgive. For what I did, was unforgivable. I will love and cherish you always forever till the very end of time, which has no end anyways, anyone knows that.

Your very best friend, soon to be someone else altogether... Marie.

Present.

FRANCESCA I did send you letters by thought.

PATSY I prayed for you, thinking you were dead or being tortured somewhere. Sitting in calculus, feeding the chickens, lying in my bed, at night, I prayed for you.

FRANCESCA I stayed in Buffalo, for six months, on the street, with a group of hippies, dropping acid and smoking hash. Then, in Albany, New York, I remember being at a boyfriend's in Albany, a much older guy, in his thirties, Gino, he was the manager of the pizzeria I worked in, and he said I could call anywhere I wanted and I dialed your number, but I hung up before it rang, I did that about twenty times.

PATSY When I come out of my coma you had already been gone three weeks. Your mother, she wouldn't open the door for me; she screamed out that the whole thing was all my fault. I was a tramp and a bad influence. I had turned you onto LSD! I went to the police and they said you were a runaway, and you were almost sixteen so there was nothing they could do.

FRANCESCA I remember sitting in a Harvey's in Buffalo, 15 years old, eating onion rings, with money I'd begged, and –knowing –deep –in –my –stomach –that nobody was... ever coming after me.

PATSY goes to FRANCESCA.

PATSY I always felt if I hadda told them.... About everything.... You know. Like what... happened, eh, then they woulda gone after you. *(FRANCESCA moves away from PATSY as the mention of "what happened" fills her with terror)* But I wasn't sure... You know, you were talking so –so –fast... And wild, you were turning in circles and.... you were, like, in a state of shock, I guess.

PATSY After what you had.... you know... or... oh.. I'm sorry. You don't want to talk about it. I just wish that you had called me, you know. I mean what... what were you... afraid of?

FRANCESCA turns away.

Scene Sixteen

Past.

The GIRLS are playing by the swings, practicing ballet moves.

PATSY Are you on welfare?

MARIE No.

PATSY Are you sure?

MARIE Yes. Who told you that?

PATSY Patty Hagerty.

MARIE She's full of shit.

PATSY I'm telling.

MARIE What?

PATSY You said the "F" word.

MARIE That's not the "F" word.

PATSY I told them that was not a nice thing to say. "If you can't say anything nice don't say anything at all". That's what my mother always says.

MARIE I am not on welfare.

PATSY I believe you.

Scene Seventeen

Present.

FRANCESCA It's nice that you can keep this house. That your mother left it to you.

PATSY Been in the family since 1816.

FRANCESCA 1816! Over a hundred and eighty years. About eight full generations, eh?

PATSY I belong in this house.

Wayne and Roger they were very upset, when Mum left the house to me they were gonna take it to court but I said to them, I said: "Listen, it was us who looked after her, me Ric and... Kevy and Ry, we were on call 24 hours a day for the last year, it was me who held her while she died, who gave her the sponge baths daily and emptied her bed pan while the two of you were busy with your "Sports Bar" in BC. They didn't even come for the last week, the final week of the woman's life. When I called 'em and I go: "she's dying and she's been askin' for you." Oh no they're too busy with the sports bar puttin' in the wide-screen TV's and that. Well in that last week before she passed on, Francesca, she was so very weak but she would sit up every now and then straight up and look at the door with these wide eyes, expecting her sons. I had to tell her they were on their way, I go "They just called and said they were on their way, Hon." That's what I said, I told her they were comin' so at least she died thinkin' her sons were on their way.

FRANCESCA I bet my mother did that. Looked at the door. For me. With her one blue eye and her brown eye.

PATSY Oh Marie. You can't know that.

FRANCESCA She used to cry. When she was drinking. Say she was no good to me.

PATSY She also used to knock you to the floor when she didn't like the look on your face.

FRANCESCA Well...

PATSY Well. *(She points to cookies)* Go on. Have another. Lunch'll be a little while.

FRANCESCA tries to eat a cookie. Puts it down.

PATSY Hah. When you were a kid, you couldn't get enough of them.

FRANCESCA I had a sweet tooth?

PATSY What? Every chance you had you'd be down at Becky's gettin' your Tootsie Roll Pops. Hah. Remember Becky's? That cat with the infected eye walkin' all over the candy? And you never saw Becky, only her daughters. She had seven daughters, remember?

FRANCESCA All of them had names starting with "B" and you never could tell them apart. "Oh hello Bettina, or is it Belinda? Nope, oh my God it's Barbara." "No, miss, I'm Betsy". Aghhhh!

PATSY Now me, I don't have a sweet tooth. I go for the chips and the cheesies. But it just seems to go right through me. You, you have the perfect figure. Well I guess you'd have to, it's your bread and butter.

FRANCESCA I think you look wonderful, Patsy.

PATSY Oh I do not, Marie, I'm a scarecrow,(or: "I'm fat") No shape on me. But it don't really matter around here. All the women are shapeless. (Or: fat.) Except the ones who are shapely. (or: "scrawny", scrawny by nature.) Shapely by nature.

PATSY Oh my Godfather I've been calling you Marie the whole time you've been here. I am sorry. Oh you must want to clobber me.

FRANCESCA No.

PATSY But you would... rather... I call you by Francesca, right? Your stage name?

FRANCESCA Well, it has been my name for twenty years. A very good friend of mine picked it for me. He died and... I don't know. I haven't been called "Marie Begg" in a very long time. And when I hear "Marie"–

PATSY You feel like Marie?

FRANCESCA Uh... yes.

PATSY And?

Scene Eighteen

Past.

The GIRLS are by the swing, each playing with a large yellow grapefruit.

PATSY Do you have lice?

MARIE No.

PATSY Yes you do.

MARIE No I don't.

PATSY I saw one. Crawling on your head. This morning. Cause you were sittin' in front of me.

MARIE You did not.

PATSY Honest. I did. I know what they look like cause my brother had them once. The Welfares brought them into the school.

MARIE I do not have lice.

PATSY I won't tell anybody, I swear, Marie. I swear on my very own life.

MARIE I don't have lice, alright?

Pause.

PATSY I could show you a special way to get rid of them. Then they would be all gone.

MARIE My mother won't buy the shampoo. She says they're not lice they're bedbugs.

PATSY That's okay. Don't you worry 'bout a THING. I'll get rid of 'em for you. I know this REALLY special way.

MARIE What's that?

PATSY I'll show you. You come over to my house, after school, okay? and I'll get rid of every single lice on your head. *(Pause)* You just come with me, after school.

PATSY Okay?

MARIE Okay.

Scene Nineteen

Present.

PATSY watches FRANCESCA's hands run over the wallpaper.

PATSY You still have those elegant hands, Francesca. You always did. Have you ever done any hand modelling?

FRANCESCA Well no, actually–

PATSY –Oh, you should go down for it. I hear you could make a fortune.

FRANCESCA Oh. Hah. Maybe I will.

PATSY You know, for the "Sunlight" commercials.

FRANCESCA Right.

PATSY We enjoyed seeing you in that commercial for the flavoured coffees.

FRANCESCA Oh that was a long time ago. I haven't done a commercial for fifteen years, Patsy.

PATSY Oh. Why is that...?

FRANCESCA Well, it's not very gratifying work and...

PATSY Looks like easy money to me.

FRANCESCA Yes. Yes it is. But....

Pause.

FRANCESCA You're not taken very seriously...if you...

PATSY Oh well you're so famous now, though.

FRANCESCA Oh, I'm not famous. Believe me.

PATSY You won all those awards. I saw it in the paper.

FRANCESCA Oh a few junky statues, yes, but they're just...for the stage, Patsy. It's the movies. Movies make you famous. And I have only made a couple of very very tiny films that about 3 people saw.

PATSY looks at her, unbelieving, full of faith in her fame.

PATSY You are being overly modest.

FRANCESCA Oh no. No. My career is definitely not what it seems to be, Patsy.

FRANCESCA wipes the kitchen table.

PATSY Well. I liked that commercial. I even went out and bought the coffee.

Pause.

PATSY I mean, I know you have done much more serious things than the commercial. I saw that one play you were in that they filmed for television. What was that?

FRANCESCA Oh. Hedda Gabler!

PATSY Yes. I liked it. Although I have to admit I did fall asleep. Well I was very tired. *(Cough)* Well now why don't I start our lunch? I have a nice chicken pot–pie and what about a Patsy salad, would you like a Patsy salad?

FRANCESCA I would love a Patsy salad.

PATSY Ric named it that he loves to tease. BIG TEASER.

PATSY begins to make lunch. There is a pie all ready to go, it has been warming in the oven. She opens some wine and sets about making a huge salad for the two of them.

PATSY Care for some ice wine?

FRANCESCA Sure. Why not?

PATSY Ric makes it himself. He is crazy about wines, got his own vintner, in Ottawa, even.

PATSY pours FRANCESCA and herself some icewine.

PATSY And... here is to...

FRANCESCA Here's to–

FRANCESCA approaches PATSY and kisses her on the cheek.

Past.

GIRLS in PATSY's bedroom singing Verse #1 of "Dark end of the Street".

GIRLS At the dark end of the Street
That is where we always meet
Hiding in shadows–

Present.

WOMEN finally clink glasses. with arms crossed.

Scene Twenty

Past.

First sleepover, PATSY is standing behind MARIE, picking nits. She wears gloves.

PATSY Seventy-nine.

MARIE Jeez.

PATSY wipes off her fingers.

PATSY Eighty.

PATSY finds another.

MARIE Holy Crow. Don't tell nobody, eh?

PATSY Eighty–one.

MARIE My mother won't do this. She says no child of hers has lice.

PATSY I don't mind doin' it. *I like it!* Eighty–two.

MARIE Sometimes, at night? I'm lyin' in bed and the itchiness is so bad I think I'm just gonna jump out a window and run down the street screaming.

PATSY looks through her hair for more nits.

PATSY And that's it for the nits. Looks pretty good. Yup. Now. Close your eyes real tight.

PATSY opens a tub of margarine.

MARIE What are you going to do? What is that?

PATSY Shhhh. It's margarine. *(mar–ja–reen)* It suffocates them.

MARIE Wait. Wait. Aren't ya gonna get in trouble for takin' the margarine?

PATSY Nope.

MARIE Are you sure... this is what ya do?

PATSY Yup.

MARIE Is it going to feel yucky?

PATSY No.

MARIE Am I going to look stupid?

PATSY No.

MARIE How long will I have to have it for?

PATSY Just till tomorrow. When we wake up. Then they'll all be dead. And then we comb'em out.

MARIE Oh the smell!

PATSY And you'll never have them again.

MARIE Never?

PATSY Never.

MARIE Never.

Scene Twenty-One

Present.

PATSY continues making lunch. FRANCESCA is drinking her ice wine.

PATSY So. I've been dying to ask you. I hope you won't think I'm nosy. Those magazines say that you have been married three times. Now I know they are always tellin' terrible lies...

FRANCESCA It's true!

PATSY No way.

FRANCESCA I know. It seems like a lot. But it just... happened that way.

PATSY Round here nobody gets divorced even. Well, Sherry Bryden, she left Norm but he was beating on her and the kids, nobody thought the less of her. And come to think of it, the Andrews. Well let's just say its not common.

FRANCESCA I thought each one was going to be forever. Except the third, which was just to help my friend Paulo get into the country.

PATSY Well now that's interesting. That you thought they were going to be forever.

FRANCESCA Hey, once a Catholic, always a Catholic. With the first, Douglas, we were so young. We had no money, we led this crazy downtown existence, living on mocha cake and Jumbo Martinis, running out of restaurants without paying, making terrible scenes in gay dance clubs, slapping people in the face, stealing lingerie from Holt Renfrew, and then being chased down Yonge Street by security, hiding in the bathroom of the Papaya Hut, gossiping viciously about everybody, passing rumours, destroying reputations. It was a lot of fun.

PATSY So what happened?

FRANCESCA Oh nothing. He turned out to be gay. I went back to school.

PATSY Gay?

FRANCESCA Uh huh.

PATSY I don't think I've ever met anyone who's gay. I mean I've seen them, on television, and in movies.

FRANCESCA Oh sure you have, Patsy.

PATSY Oh no, there's nobody gay in Marmora. I would know if there was.

Awkward moment, PATSY knows FRANCESCA thinks she is backward.

FRANCESCA Well, people can be secretive, you know. When they know they will be ...hated ...After all, no one wants to be another Marie Begg.

PATSY Oh you weren't hated.

FRANCESCA Yes I was.

PATSY I mean, it wasn't personal. You were just the scapegoat. Because you were... arty.

FRANCESCA laughs.

Awkward pause.

PATSY I've often wondered, you know, if it still bothers you, ever, when you think about it. Like, the way you were treated here, as a kid.

FRANCESCA Sometimes in a flash I am eleven years old again and they're throwing stones at me. Calling me those names and coughing. Remember? They used to cough when they saw me.

PATSY Ignorant dogs.

FRANCESCA On my bad days I think it was something in me. Something they detected? Something that is... still there. You know? There was a reason they picked on me, and not, say, Darlene Rowan, who was also poor.

PATSY Because Darlene, she knew her place, right? She never raised her head!

FRANCESCA So I walk out of my beautiful penthouse on the twentieth floor feeling this big kind of Dirty Yellow Stain all over me. The Marie Begg Stain. I go to openings, dinner parties, book launches, and I feel that people are avoiding the Stain, when they do talk to me I can feel them wanting to get away from the Stain, I see their eyes wandering and I feel the others are whispering about me, all over the room, and then I think I hear them coughing, they are coughing about me. And again, I am the girl with the running sores and the scabby legs, the lice and the dark circles under her eyes and the crooked teeth. I am Marie Begg. With the Stain.

PATSY Well you look pretty clean to me, if it's any comfort.

FRANCESCA You know its funny, I stand backstage sometimes and conjure ...their faces and I am filled with a kind of electric energy, you know? And then I go out, like a lightning bolt; I guess it's revenge. I take my revenge on the stage somehow. *(Pause)* Where are all those... people? Are they still... around?

Scene Twenty-Two

Past.

MARIE has the rain bonnet on to keep the margarine in.

MARIE Are you sure it's alright for me to sleepover?

PATSY Yeah! You heard my Mum.

MARIE She is so nice. And so pretty. This is the first time I ever been on a sleepover.

PATSY Really? How come?

MARIE Because.

PATSY I'm glad your mom said yes.

MARIE I think she was drunk. Don't tell nobody I said that. What are we having for breakfast?

PATSY French toast. With our own maple syrup.

MARIE makes the sign of the cross in gratefulness. PATSY notices.

PATSY Um Marie? I have to ask you something. Are you... um... Catholic?

MARIE What is French toast? Exactly.

PATSY I like Catholics. It's okay.

MARIE Like I know what French is. And I know what toast is.

PATSY If you're Catholic, how come you don't go to St. Mike's?

MARIE My mom said Father Duchene touched her tittie.

PATSY Shhhh.

MARIE I mean... breast. Chest.

PATSY My mom says to stay away from Catholic kids. She says they're tough. But I'll tell her you're nice... I'll tell her you don't say bad words.

MARIE I won't say no more.

PATSY Thank you.

MARIE That's why we don't have a farm anymore.

PATSY Why?

MARIE Because. We're Catholic.

PATSY Oh. That's too bad.

MARIE Because the Catholics got all the bad land. That's what my Dad says. On the other side of the 401.

PATSY So why don't you change to Protestant?

MARIE I would but I can't, you know why? Because my gramma's last words, when she was dyin' on the bed and she held on to my hand so tight I couldn't let go? Her last words to me were "Keep the Faith". And that means "Stay Catholic". And then her eyes rolled up in her head.

PATSY Ewww.

MARIE I know.

Scene Twenty-Three

Present.

PATSY So number one was " that way" who was the next husband?

FRANCESCA Oh... Paul... handsome Paul... I met him at McGill.

PATSY So what happened?

FRANCESCA We used to meet in his carrel, his study carrel? He was at the law school there. And the sex was indescribable. It even felt important, as if we were working for the French Resistance or something;

he was by far the most passionate man I had ever met but as soon as we got married, the DAY we got married he started ... to... raise his voice, no, yell at me.

PATSY No way.

FRANCESCA Just bellowed. All the time, about anything. A sock left on the floor. My dress being improper. My kissing, too hungry. And then one day, he threw a chair out the window.

PATSY Oh my god If there had been someone walkin' by with a baby in a stroller that chair coulda killed the baby.

FRANCESCA That's exactly what I told him. And then I left. Didn't want my mother all over again.

PATSY No, no ya wouldn't. *(Pause.)* What was he so damn mad about anyways?

PATSY finishes off her Patsy salad.

FRANCESCA You really want to know? That time, specifically? I cut the banana cream pie with a spoon. He found that... careless.

PATSY Hah! You used to do that around here too!

FRANCESCA I did?

PATSY Yes! Oh my Godfather, my mother would just shake her head.

FRANCESCA I don't know why I did it. I just liked to use a spoon.

PATSY laughs. FRANCESCA laughs.

FRANCESCA I just liked it!!

They laugh harder. FRANCESCA helps with the placing of the cutlery.

FRANCESCA I still do!! But I realized something, you know. I realized that in that moment, he saw Marie. When I did that. Because that is something Marie would do. Not Francesca. And he certainly did not want to be married to Marie. Who would?

PATSY Well I happen to like Marie, myself. I was disappointed when you threw away your name. Like you were throwin' my friend away, you know? I was disappointed... when you left. Did you know that?

FRANCESCA ...Lying in that hospital bed for all those weeks, with broken bones, I stared at the ceiling and I knew how I would end up if I stayed. I would end up the way they all thought of me because you can't keep fighting the way people think of you, eventually, you have to give into it, and become it: I would be the strange schoolteacher living alone. Riding a bicycle with long hair and torn stockings, being called a witch by the schoolchildren; grandchildren of the people who had thrown rocks at me, and smeared dog shit all over my coat, and thrown my books all over the yard. And that's when I decided that I was going to leave, and leave Marie behind like the Thousand Island Rat Snake leaves behind his skin, and I was never ever going to come back.

Scene Twenty-Four

Past.

GIRLS (12), by their lockers at School.

MARIE I was in the washroom today? And ya know what happened?

PATSY What?

MARIE Patty Hagerty and Jane Howard started bangin' on the door. They're bangin' on the door going, "We're going to kill you, you shitty arse face, you

Catholic whore, we're going to beat you till you shit your pants! " And I go, "My Mom already does that ANYWAYS!" I hadda stay in there the whole lunch hour.

PATSY I'm reporting them to Mr. Eaves. He'll give them the strap.

MARIE No, Patsy, don't.

PATSY But they can't keep bullying you.

MARIE Don't worry, one of these days I'm gonna come out and I'll beat their fucking faces in.

PATSY Marie. Do not use that language, please. It degrades the human body.

MARIE I'm sorry. I'm sorry Patsy, I just get so mad. I promise I won't use it anymore.

PATSY You always promise and then you–

MARIE Patsy?

PATSY Listen, Marie. I can't hang around with you if you use that kind of language. I promised my mother.

MARIE Okay. I really really won't use it again. Patsy? Patsy? Patsy?

PATSY doesn't answer. And then she suddenly turns around and hugs MARIE.

PATSY Patty and Jane? They're gonna end up workin' at the Lipton's Soup factory in Belleville, and you know that smell of powdered chicken soup? You can't get that off. Not ever.

Scene Twenty-Five

Present.

PATSY and FRANCESCA eating the meal with wine.

FRANCESCA Oh. This pastry is sublime

PATSY Actually I was kinda worried about the pastry. Thought I over-kneaded the dough.

FRANCESCA NO! And the filling...

PATSY Chicken Dijon with the red port wine, shallots and garlic, cilantro and bay leaf all grown in my garden.

FRANCESCA It's incomparable.

PATSY Gee. Alls Ric ever says is "Not bad". That is, like the height of a compliment comin' from Ric.

FRANCESCA Well he needs a shake.

PATSY Ric? Oh no, he means well.

FRANCESCA But that's not good enough. He should lavish you with praise, Patsy, you deserve it. You are his wife and he should adore you.

PATSY He likes me well enough.

FRANCESCA Likes you?

PATSY He's just not the type to say it, if you know what I mean.

FRANCESCA Patsy. Don't you get... tired? Living with the same person year after year?

PATSY No.

FRANCESCA Come on. I won't tell. I promise.

PATSY When I hear Ric's truck pullin' up? To be totally honest? I get excited, like a kid. I mix up the sound of the engine with the sound of his voice. And the truck with his body, I don't know. I like hearin' his voice, it's like warm tea goin' down my throat, and seeing like the way he rolls up his sleeves those big forearms, you know? And washes his hands, with the nails bit down, the way he sits in the chair and reads the paper while I'm makin' supper. I just like... havin' him near. It's the nearness, you know?

FRANCESCA But does he challenge you? Intellectually?

PATSY Well... he doesn't love to read the way I do, but Ric is a very smart man, Francesca.

FRANCESCA And you are equal partners?

PATSY Well of course we are. But he is the man, Francesca. And they don't tend to compromise. You know that. It's the women who tend to compromise.

FRANCESCA Patsy.

PATSY I mean I have my opinions and he listens to them, but he is the man of the household. He does usually have the final... Marie I am not one of these strident feminists who who hates men.

FRANCESCA I have never known a feminist who hates men.

PATSY Are you trying to tell me there is something wrong with my marriage?

FRANCESCA No.

PATSY Yes.

FRANCESCA Patsy. Is there any... passion left?

PATSY Passion?

FRANCESCA Yes Passion. You know.

PATSY Oh! That. Yeah. Sometimes. When the lights are out. Nosy.

FRANCESCA But, I'm talking about, you know, ecstasy? Do you find.... Ecstasy?

PATSY In sex?

FRANCESCA Well...

PATSY Not really.

FRANCESCA Then where, Patsy? Where do you find it?

PATSY I don't know. Here and there. *(Pause.)* Where do you find it?

FRANCESCA I haven't.

Scene Twenty-Six

Past.

Music.

Girls run out both holding either end of a white sheet. Pretending to be in a sleigh.

PATSY I am the beautiful Annabel Lee.

MARIE And I am the dancer, Miss Bon bon McFee.

PATSY I am wearing golden silk organza and a red rose in my hair...

MARIE And I am wearing a snow queen's dress, with the white rabbit fur and the deep blue-velvet Lake Ontario blue.

PATSY And we are on our silver sleigh...

MARIE Our sterling silver sleigh...

PATSY Going to the winter ball...

MARIE At the Marmora Castle on Marmora Hill...

PATSY And only the beautiful, the rich–

MARIE And the famous and their dogs–

PATSY There are six white horses pulling this sleigh...

MARIE And we are sipping warm hot chocolate...

PATSY With marshmallows.

MARIE The snow is deep...

PATSY And high...

MARIE Snowflakes swirl around us...

PATSY Oh!! I think it's a snowstorm, Bon bon!! Oh my heavens!

MARIE It is! It is a snowstorm! The horses are scared. *(They neigh.)* And they have lost their way.

PATSY Hours and hours and hours of cold...

MARIE The horses go way far way way WAY.

PATSY And leave us alone...

MARIE In the snow.

PATSY And I am feeling sleepy...

MARIE My eyes are getting heavy...

PATSY And I sleep...

MARIE And I sleep...

PATSY And I sleep...

MARIE And I cough...*(cough.)*

PATSY And I cough...*(cough.)*

MARIE And I freeze...

PATSY And I freeze

MARIE And they find us two days later.

PATSY Frozen stiff.

MARIE The beautiful Annabel Lee...

PATSY And BON BON McFEE.

Scene Twenty-Seven

Present

PATSY feels too warm. She gets up and looks out. She holds her head. She backs up, and looks dizzy. She leans over and breathes deeply.

PATSY Jeez, I'm finding it warm in here. Are you?

FRANCESCA Not really.

PATSY Maybe it's the stove. *(She sticks her head near an open window)* Get some air. I hope it's not the menopause. You know, with the hot flashes and that? Or maybe... You know we been tryin'... for a daughter for our old age, eh? If if if.... Come to think of it I am kinda late and.... Uh oh. Uh oh.

PATSY sees the stalker, walks backward.

FRANCESCA Patsy? Are you alright?

PATSY *(staring at the stalker)* I think so I'll just lie down. *(She lies on the kitchen chaise.)* You still know how to treat a seizure, eh?

FRANCESCA Seizure?

PATSY I know. I stole your disease on ya.

FRANCESCA Patsy? You have...

FRANCESCA gets her a drink of water.

FRANCESCA *(overlaps PATSY's first line)* Seizures?

PATSY Oh about once a month. The grand mals, just like you had.... Flailin' around, screamin' like an animal bein' slaughtered.... Last time I had one was at Kevy's Christmas recital. That was really pleasant. Oh yeah, ever since –

FRANCESCA The crash.

PATSY *(overlaps)* The crash.

PATSY I was in a coma for eight weeks, Francesca. Nothing was the same when I come out.

FRANCESCA I came, you know... to see you. Before I disappeared.

PATSY I know ya did.

FRANCESCA You knew? You knew that I was there?

PATSY nods.

PATSY I knew that you were there but I couldn't open my eyes, or my mouth. And there was something I wanted to tell you, Marie.

FRANCESCA waits.

PATSY I wanted to tell you to scratch my head. My head, my head's so itchy can you imagine an itch like the end of the world and there you were and I could not lift my hand or my arm to scratch my head and I could not move my lips or my tongue to say "Scratch" to say, "Please scratch my head" and you're standing there and I just want to sit up and scream "WILL YOU SCRATCH MY DAMN HEAD PLEASE?"

Four months in a trauma ward with angry foul talking teenaged boys who had dived off cliffs or had head on collisions!

FRANCESCA holds her.

FRANCESCA I should have stayed and helped your mother look after you, Patsy. I will never forgive myself for–

PATSY, feeling a seizure is imminent, moves away.

PATSY You should have stayed and helped my mother what? What...are you saying? To help my mother look after you? I'm sorry, I just... don't... think my mother... my...

FRANCESCA Patsy? What are you looking at, is... Patsy?

PATSY looks very frightened, and then she goes into a full epileptic seizure, hitting the floor, and convulsing. FRANCESCA at first is paralyzed, recalling her own seizures with terror. Then she goes to PATSY and holds her as she jerks. As she seizes, the lights flicker as a lightning storm, and we move to the past.

Scene Twenty-Eight

Past

Lightning storm. The 12 year old GIRLS are in a closet. Lightning and Thunder.

MARIE Patsy, my knees are killing me. How long is your Mom gonna make us stay in the closet?

PATSY Oh. Just till the lightning has passed.

MARIE How long will that be? Till the lightning passes?

PATSY I don't know. Sometimes it's all night.

MARIE Can't we just hide under the covers? In your bed? It's much more comfortable in your bed.

PATSY Marie. Kevin Creaser's aunt got killed in her bed by lightning last year. It came in the window, lightning comes in the window, get it? And do you see any windows in here? Do you?

BIG BOOM/Lightning, Thunder.

The lightning strikes, the thunder claps, the GIRLS scream. ADULT PATSY screams along as her seizure has subsided.

Scene Twenty-Nine

Present

PATSY continues screaming. Finally, she calms.

FRANCESCA Patsy? It's okay. You had a seizure.

PATSY looks around...

PATSY Oh God, I'm sorry. I'm so sorry. Here you finally come for a visit and I have to go and do that.

FRANCESCA Please, don't apologize. The important thing is that you're alright. Is there someone you would like me to call, or...?

PATSY *(feels and sees the wetness on her clothing)* OH my God how embarrassing. I'm sorry. I'm so sorry. I won't be long.

FRANCESCA Would you like some help, or...?

PATSY Oh God no, you know what it's like. Once it passes it's gone. You know that. Just I – uh could really do with some fresh air, you know? Would it be okay if we took a walk?

FRANCESCA Oh yes. Please, I would love a walk.

PATSY Good!

PATSY exits to change and shower.

FRANCESCA You know I haven't had an attack since I left here.

PATSY *(from o.s.)* Oh. That was your goin' away present, was it?

FRANCESCA looks around the room slowly. She feels dizzy herself. She falls to her knees.

Music.

Scene Thirty

The two GIRLS (12), lie on the train tracks.

PATSY Hey. I got an idea. Let's go swimmin'!

MARIE Where?

PATSY In the RIVER, silly... Look, you can see it if you really try. See? Isn't it beautiful?

MARIE Yeah. *(She does not look.)*

PATSY Well what are we waitin' for? Let's go! *(Pause.)* Well come on, Slowpokey.

MARIE I can't.

PATSY Why not?

MARIE Cause. There's eels in there. They could strangulate you.

PATSY No. No, there's no eels, just carp, ya goofus. Great big carp we feed em bread crumbs they're hardly cute! My Uncle Willy even kissed one on the lips once.

MARIE Can't go swimmin'.

PATSY Marie, I tolja...!

MARIE Don't matter bout the eels. I was just makin' that up.

PATSY Well then what then? Marie?

MARIE Promise you won't tell?

PATSY Yeah, what?

MARIE It's because uh my... secret.

PATSY What secret?

MARIE I – take... spells.

PATSY What?

MARIE Fits.

PATSY Like Darlene Rowan's brother?

MARIE Worser.

PATSY Worser?

MARIE And if, like, I did it in water I could get drownded. So, that's why I don't want to go swimmin'.

PATSY Oh boy. Can ya do it right now?

MARIE No. They just come on whenever they want to. Like a storm.

PATSY Well what are they from?

MARIE My mother hittin' me on the back of the head.

Pause.

PATSY Let's go swimmin'. Let's go swimmin' anyways.

Scene Thirty-One

Present

PATSY comes back in fresh clothes. She grabs two jackets from an outer room.

PATSY I was lookin' up on the Internet about it, eh? And did you know they used to think it was contagious? Like the common cold?

FRANCESCA Only for you and me I guess.

PATSY laughs.

PATSY Here. Put this on, you don't want to get your nice outfit covered in burrs. *(PATSY hands FRANCESCA a coat, she herself puts on Ric's coat)* And one of the cures? Was you had to drink blood flowin' fresh from a wound! Like some kind of vampire! I actually gave a talk about it at the Northumberland Epilepsy Association.

FRANCESCA Are you sure you don't want to lie down for a while before we go out?

PATSY And they used to cut off your privates! Like, genital mutilation. Thinkin' it was from bein' oversexed! Men and women, can you believe it?

FRANCESCA Patsy, are you sure you're alright? I know I used to feel very strange for *hours* afterwards. As if I were underwater. Not real.

PATSY Oh, me? I'm fine. A little embarrassed. In front of a famous person like you.

FRANCESCA Oh stop, you don't need to be embarrassed in front of me. You've seen me in seizure. I had long ones, too, twenty, thirty minutes. I remember waking up, looking into your face.

PATSY I remember your face turning purple. Like an eggplant.

FRANCESCA Cyanosis.

PATSY Right before death. That's what I always thought when I saw your face lookin' like that. That it was right before death.

FRANCESCA It was.

PATSY I know, I was holding you. Darlene Rowan's brother he did die of it. He died in the bath one Sunday, when everyone else was at church.

FRANCESCA It's funny you should mention blood because I always used to think I smelled blood before mine. This thick, dark sweet and very personal smell... you know when you wake someone up in the morning, and the smell underneath the sheets? It's the essence of the person, that smell; I guess that's why I like to sleep alone. What are they like for you, Patsy? Do you remember them at all? *(Long pause.)*

PATSY What are they like what are they like I would like to say they're like going to sleep in fact that is what I tell people, don't want to worry them, but Marie I live in fear. I live in fear of the next seizure it's like there's a stalker. And he's always there, parked in the driveway, in his old car, waiting. I come down to turn out the lights his face, in the window, his eyes, goin through me, I am out in the fields on the tractor, there he is, behind the tree, with his knife and his dirty long fingernails all for me, waiting, and sometimes, if I've had too much wine, or not enough sleep, he will walk towards me. Last week, in the Kingston Shopping Centre, there he was comin' out of the Cotton Ginny Plus store, smiling, smoking and he comes towards me and the floor starts moving and I'm lookin' around I'm saying oh my God no, no, somebody help me my God and the walls are shifting and my stomach is turning I'm about to throw up and he keeps walking towards me, he is going to kill me... Now everybody, people are staring, I put my head between my knees, "Are you alright, lady? Can I get you a glass of water?" And they don't seem to see him he is right on top of me, his scrawny arms around me his breath like vomit in my face his eyes burning me and he holds me so close like constricting, and crushing and I'm trying to yell but they can't hear my voice because he's over my face and he is pulling and pullin' me closer... can't breathe.... Can't breathe now and the people are so far away it's like he is moving me under the floor, the linoleum-marble floor and under the mall and the people and into the dark the pipes and the loneliness and they are all so far away and I will die under this floor like a cockroach all my life over, all over and he will be filled up with me and then, then, suddenly, the way someone whose been underwater just kinda pops out and the water falls off them I am there, on the floor of the mall, and the air, and the people around me, and the ambulance guys, and I sit up, I tell em it's okay, just a seizure, but I got these needles in my head, and I drink a Sprite someone's got for me, and I tell the nice lady who's a nurse that I'm okay, and the staring children, and I get myself up, and I'm shakin', yes, and wobbly, but I gotta do my shopping, gotta get it done, only come to Kingston once a month and I walk down the mall, and into the Grand and Toy, got to get supplies for the books, and he is there. There he is, behind the paper, just staring, oh he wants me back. Could be another seizure, see, that's the thing, the more you have them, the more you have them, your brain remembers that's what my doctor said, so he knows, Stalker knows he could get me again. He stands there, Marie, he stands there lickin' his dry lips, waiting, waiting with his dirty fingers to hold me too close and move me under and he knows; he knows that he can get me any time he wants.

End of Act One

Act Two, Scene One

Past

The GIRLS, 15, at the edge of the pond. They have been skating. They unlace their skates and put on their shoes.

MARIE My hands are so cold I can't feel 'em.

PATSY Mine too.

MARIE And I'm sure I have frostbite on my left ear. I don't care though. It's so nice out here.

PATSY The air.

BOTH The air... *(Laughter)*

MARIE The Ice...

PATSY Yeah....

MARIE Patsy?

PATSY Yeah.

MARIE Why do you hang around with me?

PATSY Because. You are my friend.

MARIE But what's the reason? Like...

PATSY Marie. You're always looking for reasons. Sometimes there is no reason. The only reason is that you are my friend.

MARIE But how come when you look at me, you don't see what they see? That makes them cough, and call me all those unspeakable... names.

PATSY Because, well, I didn't catch the sickness.

MARIE What sickness?

PATSY The "hate-Marie Begg"-sickness. I figure it's contagious, like a cold, eh, for stupid people. It's like, in the air and they catch it.

MARIE How come you didn't catch it.

PATSY Because.

MARIE You know, you could be a lot more popular if you didn't hang around with me. I heard that Mark Brant even thought you were cute.

PATSY Look! A falling star, look!

MARIE Quick. Say what you want to be. It'll come true if you say it on a falling star.

PATSY Ahhhhhhhhh.... Wife and mother. On the farm. Except I wouldn't have to feed the chickens. Or have anything to do with the barn.

MARIE Patsy get real. A WIFE and MOTHER?

PATSY But Marie. That's what I want.

MARIE What about a mountain climber? Or a movie star? Or a medical researcher?

PATSY Marie, you wish what YOU want. I want to be a wife and mother. That is what I want.

MARIE I don't believe you. You lost your chance.

PATSY My chance to what?

MARIE To get out of Marmora. Don't you want to get out of Marmora?

PATSY looks at her blankly.

MARIE Patsy. Do you not want to get out of Marmora? Do you want to be here for the rest of your life?

Scene Two

Present

The WOMEN are outside, up in the hay maw.

FRANCESCA My favourite place in the whole world. Ohhh the smell is glorious.

PATSY You like that? Can't stand it. Dries my sinuses right out.

They sit and look out at the farm.

FRANCESCA Patsy. I'm scared to ask... Is there anything else... Besides the attacks...?

PATSY Oh the crash left me with a big bag of bothers. Still can't move my left hand well. They call that a-taxia, can't walk fast, can't run at all, I dream about running; and you know the weirdest thing?

FRANCESCA listens.

PATSY Can't cry. Haven't cried since before the crash. Not even when Ry lost his arm, or when my Annabel was still born, I just cannot cry. Doctor says it's just one of those things.

FRANCESCA Oh Patsy, you had a stillborn baby?

PATSY I held her. For over a full day. I just held her, wrapped in the soft pink blanket my Mother had made, and I kissed her sweet little face with the white down, her toes, like Lily Of the Valley.... But I did not cry.

FRANCESCA And your son?

PATSY Yeah, well it happens, on farms. All the machinery. He was three. But he does really well with the prosthesis now, you would never know if ya saw him... Now stop lookin' like my dog after she ate the roast offa the table. As my son says, "Shit happens."

FRANCESCA I have been so... favoured.

PATSY Favoured?

FRANCESCA For me, it was a... resurrection, Patsy. Another chance. But knowing what it has done to you.. I would give anything to–

PATSY –Oh God, no, I wouldn't trade places with you for the world. NOT for the WORLD in a straw basket.

Awkward pause – FRANCESCA doesn't get it.

PATSY I mean seizures are one thing but to be haunted; the way you must be I mean I would far rather have a seizure than wake up in the night and see THEIR eyes starin' at me outa the dark. I always remember people's eyes, don't you?

FRANCESCA has a flashback of the eyes. This is very unsettling for her.

Scene Three

Past

The GIRLS are drinking parent's liquor with AM Radio in the background.

Groovy AM pop music. They are laughing hysterically.

MARIE You know what I hate?

PATSY What?

MARIE The sound of my mother going to the bathroom!

PATSY I know!

MARIE She even leaves the door open sometimes!

PATSY Oh my stars not mine she is as private as a mole. She won't even cough in front of us.

MARIE And you know what I hate even more? When she hugs me.

PATSY stops laughing.

PATSY Marie.

MARIE Last night? Calls me the Town Whore. Me! Who's never even been kissed. The Town Whore! I laughed so hard I almost puked.

PATSY Didn't your father like, defend you?

MARIE Edwin? *(Laugh)* Edwin just sits in his chair, drinking his rye and lookin' out the window for God knows what. That's why he's such a roaring success! *(Pause)* Are you sure I should crash this party? What if, like, she asks me to leave?

PATSY She won't.

MARIE How do you know? I am, like, the only person in grade eleven who wasn't invited.

PATSY Well. That's why I want you to come. To show her, if she has you at her party, that you won't ruin the party, that you can look pretty, and act cool and even get guys, just like everyone else. And anyways, there's gonna be lots of kids from St. Mike's and BCVI, they don't even know you.

MARIE Are you... sure?

PATSY Marie. Do you want to be the only one in the school sitting home tonight?

MARIE No.

PATSY Then you are crashing Cathy Corrigan's party and that's all there is to it.

Dog barking. PATSY runs to window.

MARIE You won't desert me? Once we get there?

Pause.

PATSY You know what I wish? I wish my dog would come back. She's been gone for so long.

Scene Four

Present

The WOMEN are outside, looking out at the farm.

FRANCESCA You must do very well with this farm, eh? Makin' milk for alla our milkshakes, cheese for all our pizzas.

PATSY Hey! I just heard Marie!

FRANCESCA What?

PATSY I said I just heard sweet Marie. Be careful, you might lose Francesca somewhere on the farm!!

FRANCESCA Oh get off it. So do you ever think of takin' it easy? Selling the property?

PATSY gets rubber boots.

PATSY Oh I won't tell you how much Sealtest offered us for the place.

FRANCESCA Really.

PATSY Let's just say it was SEVEN figures.

FRANCESCA Get outa town! 7! You could retire in Tahiti. Were you tempted?

PATSY For about... a day. Oh we talked about it. We argued about it. But. Well, you know....

FRANCESCA This is your life.

PATSY Here. Put these on. Don't want to step on a snake.

They put on some boots.

Scene Five

Past

MARIE and PATSY in school hallway. MARIE gives PATSY a note that the boys have passed to her.

MARIE "When I was walking all alane
I heard twa corbies making a mane.
The tane unto the tither did say,
"Whar sall we gang and dine the day?"
–In behint yon auld fail dyke,
I wot there lies a new slain knight;
And naebody kens that he lies there
But his hawk, his hound, and his lady fair.

PATSY And while you were saying this poem to the class they put this filth on your desk?

MARIE nods.

PATSY You saw them?

MARIE nods.

PATSY Why did you open it? *(Pause)* What were you thinking?

MARIE burns the note and recites –

MARIE 'Mony a one for him maks mane,
But nane sall ken whar he is gane:
O'er his white banes, when they are
bare, The wind sall blaw for evermair.'

Patsy. You don't want to know what I was thinking. You do not want to know.

MARIE puts the burning note in the trash.

Scene Six

Present

LADIES are walking on the property.

PATSY So... you're not married right now are you?

FRANCESCA No!

PATSY So you're basically single.

FRANCESCA Yup.

PATSY And do you like that? Being on your own?

FRANCESCA I love being on my own.

PATSY Do you?

FRANCESCA The peace. The FREEDOM.

PATSY I would get lonely, I think. Don't you ever?

FRANCESCA No. Never.

PATSY I don't like to be alone.

FRANCESCA Why not?

PATSY I don't know. I just go really... hairy, you know? Don't you ever....

FRANCESCA My dream, I mean a real dream I have? Is that I live by myself in the Arctic, near water, and giant shifting icebergs, surrounded by only violets and snowdrops and rough weeds, with the occasional hare racing by my little snow house, and I step out my door and see black seals in blue-green water, or walrus with their tusks, big white polar bears with Arctic Char in their mouths. And it is always just slightly above freezing? With a warm snowfall, and melting ice, and some days, when I'm very calm, I see one of those great grey sperm whales swimming by....

PATSY Still as strange as ever!

FRANCESCA Oh Yeah? You think that's strange?

PATSY Well, yes, actually, I have to say.

FRANCESCA Hey. Remember how we used to arm wrestle?

PATSY I always beat you because you had the brittle bones.

FRANCESCA Peanut brittle bones.

PATSY From malnutrition. That's what my mother always said.

FRANCESCA You think you could beat me now?

PATSY Wanna try?

FRANCESCA nods and they arm wrestle. They both try really hard. The GIRLS mirror the action. YOUNG MARIE loses to PATSY. The Women end up at an impasse.

Scene Seven

Present

FRANCESCA Oh. It's so unspeakably beautiful out here. I suppose you don't see it anymore.

PATSY I see the roof needs fixing, the rusting trailer in the back, the new machinery we haven't paid for...the hand I know is stealing from us.... Just like you when you watch a movie, you likely see the cameraman, the lights, the ropes, the make-up.... Hey, watch the fence, it's electric now.

FRANCESCA I always thought that would be a good way to go; electrocution... either by cow fence or lightning. I really like the idea of lightning.

PATSY Sometimes I don't know if you're kidding or you're serious.

FRANCESCA Oh I'm serious.

PATSY You want to die by lightning?

FRANCESCA Sometimes in a rainstorm I go for a walk. To the big park near me. No umbrella, just me, in a raincoat walking, up and down the muddy trails, over the fields.

PATSY What are you trying to do?

FRANCESCA I don't know. I think.... It's as if I need to feel that *power* again.

PATSY You mean... like... the *power of the train*? *(Pause)* You know what you need? You need a slap.

Scene Eight

Past

GIRLS (15) are in the hay mow. MARIE, in a velvet cape with a hood, is performing a Mother Goose rhyme for PATSY.

MARIE "Trip upon trenchers, and dance upon dishes, my mother sent me for some barm, some barm; she bid me go lightly, and come again quickly for fear the young men should do me some harm. Yet didn't you see, yet didn't you see what naughty tricks they put upon me? They broke my pitcher and spilt the water, and huffed my mother, and chid her daughter, and kissed my sister instead of me!"

PATSY Wow. That's really good. I think you're gonna get the part.

MARIE Thank you thank you. AND what do you have, Mademoiselle Patricia? *(She takes off her cape and wraps it around PATSY.)*

PATSY *(Pause)* I don't have anything.

MARIE Patsy. You promised.

PATSY He didn't know I'd be walking out that way. I never walk out that way this time of year. But I was walkin' out that way so I could practice my rhyme. It was the one about these girls? Skating in the summer? And falling through the ice and so I wanted to go way far out so Roger and Wayne wouldn't make fun of me–

MARIE Patsy?

PATSY And I'm walkin' near the raspberry bush? You know where we get all the raspberries for Mum's pies? And this smell almost knocked me over and I hear the flies buzzin' so loud and I look and I seen this... black and white thing, like, tied to the tree and the sound of the flies it's like they are inside my ear and I plug my nose and I go closer and when I seen her I threw up. I couldn't stay to bury her, because I kept gagging on the smell–

MARIE –It was Belle? It was Belle, and she was dead? Patsy?

PATSY See I figure he had to tie her to the tree, because otherwise she would run away when she heard the shot and he would have to shoot her again, and maybe he would just wound her, and then he would have to shoot her again, and she would have such terrible fear, and my Dad cares for dumb animals he does, so he had to tie her to the tree. And my Dad does not have the time to lift her and put her in the truck and take her down to the dump he is very busy he has to work the farm so he had to leave her there.

MARIE You found her? You found her tied to a tree? Shot dead?

PATSY nods.

MARIE But why did he shoot her, Patsy?

PATSY She was nipping the cattle. And that spoils the milk. I remember him saying, "If she nips at them again..." but I didn't really.. Ya see when cattle get scared; it spoils their milk. My dad had no choice.

MARIE But couldn't he... have... just....

PATSY Don't you listen? Don't you know ANYTHING? *I said he didn't have any choice*! Now leave me alone!! Just LEAVE ME ALONE!!

Scene Nine

Present

The WOMEN are by the pond.

PATSY Remember this pond?

FRANCESCA We used to skate on it.

PATSY That's right.

FRANCESCA And skinny dip. Summer nights.

PATSY Ric and I, we still do. We love it.

FRANCESCA I wonder if your mother and father did too?

PATSY My mother? Oh no. She was as private as a mole. I couldn't imagine my mother ever taking her clothes off, even for a bath, let alone...you know it's funny, when my mother was dying her belly was all swollen, eh, from the fluid? And she's lying there, barely able to speak, eh, and she takes my hand and she says to me: "I'm feeling too sexy". I'm like, "What? Too salty? Want some water?" And she's like "No" she's gettin' frustrated. It took me about ten minutes to understand what she was saying, eh. And I'm like, "You say you're feeling too sexy, Mum?" At first I thought she was just losin' her mind, but then after about a day I got out of her that her insides were like pressin' down on her vagina somehow, right? And causin' her to feel, like aroused. Alla the time.

FRANCESCA just shakes her head.

PATSY I just felt so very bad when she told me that. It seemed like a very bad joke or something, right? Her being such a lady.

FRANCESCA Yeah, but what's wrong with a lady feeling sexy?

PATSY It's just not... dignified.

FRANCESCA I would love to die feeling sexy.

PATSY Without having any control, like a barn cat in heat?

FRANCESCA Yes.

PATSY I don't believe you.

FRANCESCA That's the way I live. Why shouldn't it be the way I die?

PATSY Highly sexed, are ya? Hah. I have a girlfriend like that. Lorraine. We tease her.

FRANCESCA Many of us are like that, Patsy. Many women...

PATSY I wouldn't care to be like that.

FRANCESCA And why not?

PATSY Because. I like to be in control of my feelings.

FRANCESCA Are you, maybe, afraid?

PATSY Afraid? Of what?

FRANCESCA Of... your own... passion? I mean, isn't that, in a way, why you have never left... Marmora?

PATSY No. I don't THINK so, but I could be wrong. I mean what would I know about myself? What are you talkin' about "never left" Francesca? I went to Kingston, didn't I go to Queen's for two years in occupational therapy where I won a scholarship for further study, which I turned down? I have been on trips with Ric here and there to Toronto, to Montreal, to Vermont. One time we even went on a Caribbean cruise once. I leave SOMETIMES. It is you who never left, Marie. I mean look: Just look at your face.

FRANCESCA touches her face/cheek, as MARIE mirrors the action in the next scene {Acne Cysts}.

Scene Ten

Past

GIRLS in kitchen. MARIE is burning her face with boiled water in a bowl, and washcloth. PATSY walks in with fresh eggs in a basket.

PATSY What are you doing? Marie. What are you doing?

MARIE Burning my face.

PATSY BURNING your face? May I ask why?

MARIE To kill the acne cysts.

PATSY Marie. Did your doctor say that was okay?

MARIE If I burn it, I kill the infection, see?

PATSY But... *(MARIE shows her under the cloth)* Oh my God. Oh my God Marie don't do that again. You hear me?

MARIE Patsy, you don't understand. I would rather have this big burn on my face, which then scabs, and bleeds and everything, than have the acne. Because with the acne, it's like alive, you can feel the bacteria crawling under your skin. And you know how that makes me feel?

PATSY tries to grab washcloth.

MARIE Patsy. I need to do this.

PATSY No.

MARIE Give it to me.

PATSY No. Not in my house. You are not burning your face in my house. I like your face, Marie. And I don't want you to burn it.

Scene Eleven

Present.

On the property.

PATSY I mean, let's be honest, there, Francesca. Aren't you the one who's afraid?

FRANCESCA Of what?

PATSY Well you haven't had any children, now have you?

FRANCESCA That was a carefully considered choice, Patsy.

PATSY Really?

FRANCESCA Yes. There are many good reasons:

PATSY Well. I suppose it is a lot of work.

FRANCESCA It's not that.

PATSY No?

FRANCESCA I'm not afraid of work.

PATSY Okay, then what is it?

FRANCESCA Well for one thing I travel.

PATSY You could bring a nanny along–

FRANCESCA Patsy!

PATSY I think you are scared. I think you are scared because children always see who you really are. And your child would see right through the fancy Francesca to my sad and lonely sweet Marie.

FRANCESCA Oh come on I'm not so fancy now. And I wasn't just sad and lonely then.

PATSY I just wouldn't want you to miss out, Marie.

FRANCESCA I don't feel as though I've missed out.

PATSY But you have. To be perfectly honest you have REALLY missed out. Big time.

FRANCESCA YOU have missed out, Patsy. By staying here, in this closed and narrow little community, on this farm, hunkering down like a scared rabbit. Really. A couple of trips here and there is nothing. There's a whole world out there. An unimaginable world.

PATSY Yeah? Like what? What is so unimaginable?

FRANCESCA The underground cave cities in Turkey. The 13th century golden roof in Innsbruck, Austria, with the alps behind it.... The Tower of London, The Wailing Wall in Jerusalem, Stonehenge!

PATSY Alright. I admit it. I have missed out. Somewhat.

FRANCESCA You see?

PATSY But *you* have missed out more.

Scene Twelve

Hay Maw. GIRLS, 15. Brushing the dog poop off MARIE's coat.

MARIE If somebody would just tell me why they are doing this to me, I would be their slave for life if somebody would just tell me what is WRONG with me. I know I'm not UGLY, aside from my face, I do really well in school, I'm nice, I mean what the hell is wrong with me?

PATSY Nothing.

MARIE Nothing? You promise, nothing?

PATSY Well, maybe, I don't know.

MARIE What?

PATSY Nothing.

MARIE No, what?

PATSY Well.

MARIE Please. Please, Patsy.

PATSY Well. Maybe... if you had... a....

MARIE What? *(Long pause)*

PATSY Bath?

MARIE What?

PATSY I mean, no offense or anything, and it doesn't bother me at all, but I was just thinking that maybe if you like, took a bath or a shower more.

MARIE Are you saying... I smell?

PATSY No. Just a little. Sometimes.

MARIE I smell? Really? But I wash under my arms with soap every day. I couldn't smell. You're crazy.

PATSY shrugs.

MARIE Patsy? *(Pause)* Why didn't you tell me this before?

PATSY shrugs.

MARIE What...what does it smell like?

PATSY shrugs.

MARIE Like Linda Perchuk? Not like Linda Perchuk?

PATSY My mom says that when a girl gets her period–

MARIE What?

PATSY That well, when you reach puberty all these strange smells start to happen and well that you need to take a bath once a week.

MARIE Do you? Take one once a week?

PATSY My Mom makes us.

MARIE Once a week?

PATSY Every Saturday night Mum fills up the bath That takes an hour or two and then all five of us take a bath so we'll be nice and clean for church on Sunday. I always go first cause I'm the cleanest.

MARIE slaps herself. PATSY tries to stop her, grabs MARIE in a hold/embrace.

PATSY Don't Marie. Stop that. Marie!! ...I'm sorry. I shouldn't have....

MARIE See the thing is... I want to take a bath, right. I wanted to take a bath like every ten days. But the last time I filled the bath my Mum gave me a black eye cause we don't have any water see cause we don't hardly have any water in our well, we – Is that Mud Lake? Near those trees?

PATSY Yeah, that's Mud Lake.

MARIE We should walk out there one day.

PATSY No.

MARIE How come?

PATSY It's weedy. Brian Ring's cousin from Gan he died in it.

MARIE Not to swim in it, just to see it.

PATSY You can't even put a boat in it.

MARIE Just to see it, Pats. Don't you want to see it?

PATSY My mother, she grew up here and she's never seen it.

Scene Thirteen

Present

WOMEN are out by the lake.

FRANCESCA My last long affair was with a family man. He had four children and he... turned away from them. The constant whining and sickness, the terrible nasty fighting, the unceasing sound of the television, the demands for money, and the latest toy, and fashion, he wanted away. And when he left them for me, he felt no remorse. We lived in a beautiful glass house, by a river; They would phone, crying, begging, and he would calmly tell them he had made up his mind. I found that very... discouraging, somehow.

PATSY So what happened to him?

FRANCESCA Oh. I got bored with him. After the thrill of breaking up a family wore off.

PATSY The thrill...?

FRANCESCA I'm not proud of it.

PATSY Well. I'm sure you wouldn't do it again.

FRANCESCA I probably would.

PATSY If you did it to me I'd come after you with a baseball bat.

FRANCESCA And I would deserve it.

Pause.

FRANCESCA Patsy? I am afraid! I am afraid... that I would give birth to Marie Begg. You know? Do you know what I mean?

FRANCESCA screams, she sees a snake close by.

PATSY What is it? Is it a snake? I know how you feel, I've been livin' with them all these years and still whenever I see one I feel the way I did when Keith Knight punched me in the stomach.

FRANCESCA I seem to be having trouble breathing. I don't know.

PATSY It's just a garter. They are a nuisance but they're not at all poisonous honest, you don't need to worry–

FRANCESCA Can you help me breathe?

PATSY Breathe?

FRANCESCA Would you please... help... me breathe?

Nancy Palk (top) and Sonja Smits.

Photo by Cylla von Tiedemann

PATSY Are you... do you have asthma or...? Okay... okay... Marie... I want you to breathe in as I count to four, just deep and slow, got it? Okay 1-2-3-4 and out to the count of 4, here we go, 1-2-3 and 4. That's a girl.... Feelin' better? Tell me, hon', you just tell me what you're feelin'.

FRANCESCA I'm feelin'....

PATSY Are you...?

FRANCESCA I don't know, I'm falling apart here.

PATSY holds FRANCESCA in silence, GIRLS sing Dark end of the Street.

Scene Fourteen

The two girls in PATSY's bed, sleeping over. They could be smoking. They sing in harmony.

GIRLS At the dark end of the street
That's where we... always meet.
Hiding in shadows
Where we don't belong
Living in darkness to hide our wrong.
You and me
At the Dark End of the Street
You and me...

PATSY Peter Butler is the most beautiful kisser in this country. He's way better than Ric.

MARIE What's it like? I can't even imagine.

PATSY Kissing? it's like it's like... okay, you know last Sunday when we made strawberry ice cream by hand?

MARIE Yeah.

PATSY And the cream is in the cold salty steel and you're churning it round and round with that big steel spoon and then ya pour in the strawberries and the red juice runs through the cream and turns it deep pink and it's gettin colder and churning and if you put your face in right into the churning ice cream at that moment when it's goin' pink with the red juice and turning from cream to ice cream.. THAT... is the moment of a kiss.

MARIE I want to kiss like that.

PATSY You will.

MARIE Not while I live in Marmora.

PATSY That's ridiculous.

MARIE I'm the town dog, Patsy. *(MARIE barks.)*

PATSY Stop it. That is not true.

MARIE My mouth aches, it aches, Patsy, from wanting to kiss.

PATSY Who? Who do you want to kiss, Marie?

MARIE Nobody.

PATSY Come on, you can tell me.

MARIE Nobody.

PATSY Donny Neilson?

MARIE is quiet.

PATSY The shy one? Goes to St. Mike's?

MARIE He talked to me today. At the free skate.

PATSY No way. I've never seen him talk to a girl.

MARIE He was talking about how he plays hockey. How he plays every day for hours and hours practicing his shot, just like Bobby Orr did when he was growing up; he says he's got the best shot in the province and he's gonna play for the Kingston Frontenacs, and then for the Montreal Canadiens. He said he dreams about hockey.

PATSY He said all of that? To you?

MARIE nods.

PATSY Well, the Sadie Hawkins dance is comin' up. Why don't you ask him?

MARIE No way.

PATSY Marie.

MARIE No. Way.

PATSY Marie! I'm gonna call him, and–

MARIE Patsy. If you do that, I will never forgive you.

PATSY Promise me you'll think about it.

MARIE I am not promising anything. Now let me go to sleep.

PATSY "Says the little girl to the little boy, What shall we do? Says the little boy to the little girl, I will kiss you!!!!!"

Present

ADULT PATSY sings (refrain) 1st verse of "Dark end of the Street".

PATSY At the dark end of the street
That's where we.... always meet.
Hiding in shadows
Where we don't belong
Living in darkness to hide our wrong.
You and me
At the dark end of the street
You and me...

FRANCESCA Patsy, let's go to the tracks. I want to go to the train tracks.

Scene Fifteen

Past

Getting ready for the dance. PATSY hairsprays MARIE's hair, takes out hair rollers.

AM radio music.

PATSY Now, with the mascara, you brush over the eyelashes three times and then under'em three times. And you have to wipe the wand off eh? So it doesn't get all goopy and make you look like white trash.

MARIE Are you sure the blue mascara isn't too much?

PATSY Oh everybody's wearin' the blue. And with the baby blue eyeshadow, it's gorgeous. Oh my god your hair is perfect, you look like Miss America ..it's shimmering..

MARIE Like Ice.

PATSY Oh now make sure it falls over your shoulder, just so, it makes guys go insane with desire.

MARIE goes to touch it.

PATSY Now don't touch it.

MARIE goes to touch it.

PATSY DON'T TOUCH it.

MARIE I wish you were coming.

PATSY Oh this flu is so bad I can hardly see straight. Anyway, Ric's been weird lately, I'm playing hard to get.

MARIE What do I do if he kisses me, Patsy?

PATSY You just kiss back. But gently. Don't put your tongue in his mouth till he puts his in yours. And above all do not let him feel you up.

MARIE How come?

PATSY Marie. You know what they think of sluts around here. Look at Darlene Rowan.

MARIE Yeah.

PATSY You just slap his hand, hard. And make sure everybody sees ya.

MARIE has finished her makeup, shows her face.

MARIE How's that? Is that okay?

PATSY Beautiful.

MARIE Are you sure?

PATSY Yes I'm sure. You can hardly even notice your boils. Especially when your hair falls over them.

PATSY gets the dress.

PATSY And now.... *(She makes a horn sound like a fanfare)* Da Da Da Da!

She puts the dress on MARIE. It looks beautiful. We can see the beautiful woman she will become.

MARIE Is it alright?

PATSY *(takes her to a mirror)* You are gonna be the prettiest girl at the dance. And they're all gonna go like, "What happened to Marie Begg? I mean like where is Marie Begg?"

Scene Sixteen

Present

The railroad tracks come into view.

PATSY Recognize these?

FRANCESCA Oh yes. Oh yes.

PATSY Still comes by here, three times a day.

FRANCESCA Smells. Oh my God. That smell.

PATSY Yeah. Well. You know what that is. That's sewage, eh? They just dump it, right on the tracks.

FRANCESCA is going into pre–seizure mode. She is there, and not there.

FRANCESCA *(coughs)* ohhh. *(Deep breath)* Ohhhh. Oh... oh... oh... that was me, that was how I smelled, after the dance; (*She starts wiping it off, trying to dry herself)* I couldn't wash it off, you know? I tried, in the sink at the Tim Hortons, with lots and lots of that pink creamy soap but the smell it wouldn't come off, it just got stronger and stronger and I was so dizzy from the fumes I never told anyone I never told anyone about that, not even you but you could smell it. Couldn't you?

It was dark when it happened, wasn't it?

PATSY Yes, I believe it was. It was dark.

FRANCESCA But the air was fresh.

PATSY That's right.

FRANCESCA I had worn that green dress you made me–

PATSY Yes you did.

FRANCESCA And the white lace stockings....

PATSY And I had brushed your hair until it shimmered–

FRANCESCA –Like Ice....

PATSY You looked beautiful.

FRANCESCA I looked beautiful. Except for the shoes with the broken heel– I was hoping no one would notice the shoes it was spring; white tulips tall, burgundy spray all over the sidewalks and the yellow forsythia everywhere and maples about to burst and the fragrance, the fragrance; I waited for him on the steps of the Kentucky Fried Chicken and then there he was, his hair combed. His hands clean we didn't say a word, we walked and he actually held my hand, our hands were both sweating, I almost fainted with desire I had never been touched you see, by a boy I wanted to fall into the grass with him so we walked to the school, we went into the gym with the streamers and the punch bowl and the band was playing *(she sings)* "smile a little smile for me, Rose Marie", he was still holding my hand, but the others, Pat Letour and Roly and them, they looked and they stared and after a while, they they started to cough they were laughing at him and there was that moment when he knew he was being laughed at... THE COUGHING... because of me. And the coughing. He suddenly knew I was the school dog he hadn't realized, you see, COUGHING... because he was from St. Mike's, so so he turned white white like the tulips ... he shook off my hand and and and....

PATSY is wary, but with her.

PATSY And then what, Marie? What happened then?

FRANCESCA He never came back. I waited by the wall and I waited and they stared and they gathered and they threw spitballs and he never came back. I heard his car drive away I knew the sound of his car. I walked out my head down my legs shaking across the football field. In my mother's high heels and and *(PATSY helps her)*

PATSY Do you want to go back, hon, we could go back.

FRANCESCA And they were suddenly there, Pat, Roland, Mike and Jamie and they pushed me from behind, and then from the front and they were laughing. And saying my hair looked nice. And wouldn't it look nice with sperm all over it. I didn't understand that.. And I started to feel sick, sick to my stomach... and in my head like I was going to have a seizure. And all their hands, their fingers, touching me.. I tried to walk past them. But someone grabbed my arms. So hard. They were all around me and there wasn't a space no space. They kept laughing. And coughing. And moving closer and closer. Their saliva spraying on my face and saying dirty words, filthy words I didn't understand. And then I fell backwards, on my back and them all unzipping their pants and then wham! I went into seizure in and out and when I would come out for a moment I would feel the spraying on my face, and see their faces, the sound, the spraying, the SMELL ohhhhhh Patsy the SMELL....

FRANCESCA collapses in PATSY's arms ...she relives the memory.

Scene Seventeen

Past

AM radio music.

While listening to pop music on the radio, PATSY is making an apple pie, keeps her back to MARIE who enters the kitchen, her pretty dress a mess. The back is all muddy as if she lay on the dirt. The front is very wrinkled and ripped. There is blood, also on the back. She is shaking uncontrollably and her teeth are chattering.

MARIE Patsy?

PATSY How was it? Gimme all the dirt. I want every detail. Did ya dance a slow dance? Tammy phoned and said the band really sucked, and my Ric was there with *Gerette Blanchard*. I will never speak to her again I am so glad I have the flu. Temperature's 104 I'm not kiddin' you. But I gotta do these pies for Mum, she's serving them to... Holy God. What happened to you?

MARIE cannot answer. She sits down, trembling, shaky. She has picked up a partially smoked wet butt off the road....

MARIE Do you...have a light?

PATSY approaches her. MARIE smells terrible, of urine. She is having trouble breathing and therefore trouble speaking. When she speaks it is as if she is winded, without breath.

PATSY Aww. *(She gags)* Marie!?

MARIE Will ya give me a light...?

PATSY Marie, have you peed your pants Marie? Listen, do you... want to see a doctor?

MARIE No.

PATSY Well what's going on will you please tell me? You didn't take some of that acid they're passin' around the school?

MARIE No.

PATSY Marie. What happened to you?

MARIE goes to the sink and pours water over her head and washes, washes.

PATSY You are stoned. You are stoned and you're havin' a bad trip. I'm takin' you to hospital.

MARIE No. No hospital. No.

PATSY Marie. You're shaking. Did you get hit by a car or something? Where's Donny? Did he drop you off here?

MARIE I walked from town.

PATSY You walked! That's ten miles, Marie. Look at you, you're barefoot, where are your shoes, where are your shoes, Marie?

MARIE Is it true about Holly French?

PATSY What?

MARIE That she does that...

PATSY What?

MARIE All the time. She does that all the time.

PATSY WHAT?

MARIE With all of them.. By the goalpost. That's what they said.

PATSY I do not know what you are talkin' about, Marie and I'm sure Holly French wouldn't neither. Now come on, I'm putting' you in the car and I am takin' you to the doctor.

MARIE walks in circles round the room, speaking the following in a low continuous mutter.

MARIE She she does it all the time she does that all the time all the cute girls do. All the cute girls do; the cheerleaders, gymnastic team, really really you gotta trust us: Okay, are you sure? Is that true? Really is that true that all the cute girls do this? Holly French, and Carol O'Roarke and Nancy Tanks they all do this? Really I don't believe you guys, you guys are teasing me. Oh yeah yeah, baby, promise promise on my mother's life that's what he said *On My Mother's Life*, right here by the goalpost every dance Holly and Carol and

Liisa Repo-Martell (left) and Tara Rosling.

Photo by Cylla von Tiedemann

Nancy all the cute girls, we'll be gentle come on, you are so pretty we'll be gentle so pretty in that green dress. Me pretty? With my face? Then why did Donny take off like that? Oh he's an asshole we can see what a pretty face underneath, you're a good looking girl we have always liked your legs... such nice long legs let us see your legs pull up the dress. That's right nice knees pull it up way up oh yes oh yes and your hair such beautiful hair would look so nice with sperm in it.. EH? EH? EH? What's sperm? What's sperm? You can come to all our games now, Marie, and party after, go for pizza sit with us at lunch instead of all by yourself or with Patsy.... She's so straight, you're not straight like her... after the games we party hard we party hard over at Dave's.... Would you like to come with us and party ...hard? "YOU DOG TURN OVER YOU DOG. I'LL SCREW YOU TO DEATH"

HAH HAH HAH and barking and coughing and barking... and Michael and Roland and Jamie and Frank and "TURN OVER BITCH".

BY THE THROAT, by the HAIR, by the GOAL-POST!

And the moon was so low and so big and so yellow.

PATSY is silent, devastated.

Scene Eighteen

PATSY is holding FRANCESCA.

PATSY Are you alright?

FRANCESCA I don't know. I don't know.

PATSY I think we should go back now it's getting dark.

FRANCESCA Is the train coming, Patsy? Is the train coming soon?

Silence.

Scene Nineteen

Past.

PATSY is chasing MARIE, just outside of the house.

PATSY Marie!! Wait up, wait up! MARIE. Where are you going? MARIEEEEE!! I'm freezing. My pie's in the oven. For God's sakes, wait up! Marie, where ya goin'?

MARIE climbs up the hill to the railroad tracks.

PATSY Marie you are not thinkin' of doin' something stupid are ya?

MARIE I'm waiting for the train, Patsy.

PATSY Train doesn't stop here, Marie. Only stops in Belleville.

MARIE It will stop for me.

PATSY Marie, did you get hit on the head?

MARIE I'll take the train to the ocean. As far from here as I can go.

PATSY You are goin' mental, Marie, I swear to God if you could hear yourself.

MARIE Goin' away now. Away from here.

PATSY Marie, if you don't get down from there the train is going to hit you.

MARIE The train will stop for me. It will stop for both of us, Patsy. Come on, come with me.

PATSY Marie. I don't know exactly what you were talkin' about back there, but it sounded to me like those boys... were botherin' you. Were they botherin' you? Cause I will call the cops on them, Marie.

MARIE Their eyes their eyes like rats.

PATSY Just come on down from here and we'll go to the police. It's the right thing to do, Marie.

PATSY reaches for MARIE arms outstretched. She is crying.

MARIE Patsy?

PATSY goes to her and they embrace.

PATSY Oh baby.

MARIE I'm scared.

PATSY Me too, Marie. You're acting so strange.

MARIE Come with me. We have to get away from here, come with me.

PATSY I can't. I can't, Marie. This is my home.

MARIE I'm going to walk and walk along the tracks until I get somewhere else, that's what I'll do.

PATSY Now now, ya can't do that, it's dangerous.

MARIE Come with me, Patsy.

PATSY Marie you come offa this track. I think I hear something.

Present

ADULT PATSY And I'm standing behind you and I'm sayin' "You get right down offa here, Marie." I think I hear something.

MARIE My best friend. Will you come with me? Please?

(left to right) Nancy Palk, Tara Rosling,
Liisa Repo-Martell and Sonja Smits.

Photo by Cylla von Tiedemann

PATSY And I know my damn pie is burning Marie, it's my mother's pie for her luncheon tomorrow you are not makin' sense if you don't come offa that track you're not goin' anywhere. Oh my God the PIE IS BURNING!

The sound of the train grows. A rumble.

MARIE stretches her hands towards the direction the train will be coming from. PATSY gets off tracks and tries to pull MARIE off.

ADULT PATSY And, and the train is coming, I can feel it in my feet and I pull... and I pull... wanna save my friend... wanna save my friend and then... and then..... and I can't explain it.. I guess maybe it was my temperature of 104, and my thinking was muddled but suddenly I looked at that moon and I thought, "Yeah. Me and Marie, me and Marie.

YOUNG PATSY gets back on tracks behind MARIE, embraces her.

ADULT PATSY "We are gonna die beautiful, we are gonna get crashed by the train and then fly through the sky."

ADULT PATSY And I felt this deep yearning, Marie this yearning for for for nothing I could ever name, you know? Because there is just there is just no word for it and and I held your hand so cool and sweaty and we are holding hands together and we will become the TRAIN and the smell of the pie, and the pie is burning and oh orange light! And YOU are pullin' on me *(MARIE's thinking clears, she gets off tracks and tries to pull PATSY off.)* pullin' away but I am not gonna let you go I am stronger than you farm strong. I am going to stay on this track then I feel it I feel it in my feet and your fingernails diggin' in I am the train I am big I am metal! I am moving so fast I am—

The Crash.

Scene Twenty

Present

PATSY Flying. We flew. Through the air...

FRANCESCA We flew. Through the air... Are you saying that I ...saved *your* life? Patsy?

PATSY You saved my life... but you always had... saved my life, Marie. Ever since we were little girls.

FRANCESCA Really? Is that true?

PATSY Ever since you looked at me. With those eyes, like the bottom of Mud Lake. And spoke, with your mouth, all those thoughts. You will never... know.

FRANCESCA Oh my God. Patsy.

PATSY Marie. I am so sorry. You feeling guilty all these years. Did I say I was sorry?

FRANCESCA No no no we were there together and we both wanted to fly away, that's all we wanted, to – fly away, to –

The WOMEN make it back to the kitchen area.

FRANCESCA Oh Patsy. What a day.

PATSY That's for sure.

FRANCESCA God. You know right now? I wish I could stay forever.

PATSY Me too. But you can't, I suppose. Hey. It must be at least five, sun's almost down.

FRANCESCA Oh. I wish I could just stay – for a few days.

PATSY Well go ahead. Stay. Phone and tell'em you've got the stomach flu.

FRANCESCA I'm tempted.

PATSY You could meet Ric and the boys, ride the horses, sample all my different pies, we could look at old pictures, come on.

FRANCESCA Well... no, I can't. I can't disappoint them.

PATSY Marie. Is there ...really... this gala happening?

FRANCESCA takes off boots and puts on her own shoes.

FRANCESCA Of course there is, it's for a film I made a while ago, it's... there really really is, Patsy.

PATSY begins to make her ball of dough.

PATSY That's okay. I do it sometimes, like we'll be visiting Elizabeth Ryan and I'll say I gotta get back and take my roast out, and I don't even have a roast.

FRANCESCA Well I honestly do have an engagement. I could show you the invitation. But you are right, that even if I didn't... I don't know....

PATSY You'd be afraid.

FRANCESCA Yes.

PATSY That if you stay too long.

FRANCESCA I might never leave.

PATSY And you would lose Francesca.

FRANCESCA I have lost Francesca.

PATSY Hooray. Are you gonna go back to Marie Begg?

FRANCESCA I'm not Marie Begg either.

PATSY Is this all good?

FRANCESCA embraces PATSY from behind; they hang onto each other with all their love and history, and even desperation. Slowly, FRANCESCA extricates herself and backs out of the set, looking at PATSY until she disappears.

PATSY We aren't going to see each other again, are we, Marie...? We aren't going to see each other ever again. It's going to be like you were never here. Like you were a dream. I'll be sitting here six months from now and making my pastry and the snow will be falling and this afternoon will all seem... unreal.

FRANCESCA I will think about you every day.

PATSY And I'll be looking at that snow and I will feel the pastry dough in my hands and I will knead it and knead it until my hands they are aching and I think I'm like making you. I like... form you; right in front of my eyes, right here at my kitchen table into flesh. Lookin' at me, talking soft.

FRANCESCA disappears.

The GIRLS are gone. Sound of a train. PATSY raises her hand.

PATSY I will not forget you. "You are carved in the palm of my hand."

Slow fade to black.

The End

OTHER TITLES BY JUDITH THOMPSON

Lion in the Streets
Winner, Floyd S. Chalmers Canadian Play Award for Drama, 1991.
PLCN (tpb) 0-88754-515-7 (1997) $ 13.95

The Other Side of the Dark
Includes "The Crackwalker", "I Am Yours", "Pink", and "Tornado" (radio).
PLCN (tpb) 0-88754-537-8 (1997) $ 18.95

Sled
Nominated, Governor General's Literary Award for Drama, 1995.
PLCN (tpb) 0-88754-517-3 (1998) $ 14.95

White Biting Dog
Winner, Governor General's Literary Award for Drama, 1984.
PLCN (tpb) 0-88754-369-3 (1984) $ 10.95

White Sand (radio)
In *Airborne*
BLI (pb) 0-921368-22-4 (1991) $ 14.95